DIMITRIOS MISTRIOTIS

IT ARCHETYPES

PUBLISHED IN

2018

PROOF READ BY

Christos Tsilopoulos
(Chapters 01, 02, 03, 04, 06, 07, 08, 09, 10)

William Taylor
(Chapter 13)

George Klontzas,
'Momentum' School Of English Language
(Chapters 02, 03, 04, 05, 06, 09, 10, 11, 12)

Mark Smith
(spelling corrections)

DESIGNED BY

Harris Rodis

TEXT SET IN

Source Code Pro, Freight Sans Pro

Copyright © 2018 by Dimitrios Mistriotis

CONTENTS

7   Introduction

PART 1 – THE PEOPLE

16   Personality Archetypes

22   Commandos

28   Infantry

34   Police

40   How They See Each Other

PART 2 – GAMES PEOPLE PLAY

48   The Companies

58   One to Ten Gentrification

66   Policemen Killing Machine

70   Programming Languages as Archetype & Culture Indicators

78   Ad postings - The 10 Years of Rails Experience

83   Teams

PART 3 – ESSAYS

90   Spaniards & Englishmen, Mindsets, and Black Boxes

99   Commando for Ever / Alternative Company Structures

108   Why Google?

116   Bibliography

INTRODUCTION

THERE ARE NOW *more than 7.2 billion people on planet Earth. About 32 million of them visit Stack Overflow monthly...*[1] which would categorise them as "developers". Living in an era defined by software where *"Software is eating up the world"*, some of us might wonder about who all these people are? What motivates them on a personal and professional level, why and how do they operate? Are they all or most of them obsessed "Geeks"?, Do they secretly admire Mark Zuckerberg? Why do some of them bring up questions about Spolsky test in interviews and what is a "Spolsky test" anyway?

MOTIVATION

The decision to start writing about the above sparked from personal experiences. Some years before circa 2013 I started working for a company whose whole infrastructure and culture was stuck about fifteen years in the past. The

---

[1]. Source: http://stackoverflow.com/research/developer-survey-2015

moment I realised what was going on, just after the induction, I wanted to leave. I eventually lasted there a little more than a year, having endured a number of panic attacks and similar episodes in between. While being in that company I was constantly wondering if is there something wrong with me, If I cannot stand being here then why are all these people around me happy - some of them so happy - with their jobs? Or if not leaning towards happyness, why do they not seem so upset? Later on I entertained Could it be that I am right and they are wrong? What if we have different perspectives? And more important, should I try adjust to working with arcane technologies or leave the company and take my chances somewhere else?

I was always reading technical materials and books about the sociology of software. The experiences in that company accelerated the reading process, made me start checking out all the related material I would encounter. Later on continued with compiling my thoughts to what eventually grew up to become this book. Along the way I started to believe that people on the IT profession have different motivations, career aspirations, targets, and probably life approaches. Could the person that contributes to the development of say Microsoft's Word or Excel in the mid 90s have the same aspirations and attitude towards his job as a person who successfully maintains a big company's payroll application for twenty years? Yet in many publications people of the field are treated as a homogeneous population an approach that directly contradicts my observations. Could something closer to the recently popularised "tribe" model explain some of the differences while filling the gaps of existing literature?

Along the way some questions started to bug me some of them around the people on the field and how they see their profession and the rest of the world. Also there used to be many publications on how the world sees and conceptualises us, "Geeks", "Nerds", the whole IT sector in general. It was very common to read or listen from a sociologist, a psychologist, or just a journalist trying describe the culture and norms with the tools that his discipline provides. The pattern is usually similar to the university professor who after living some years along a tribe in the depths of the Amazon river, gets back to share his observations. Would it not be interesting if we tried to apply a reverse approach? Such as asking the IT native in this case to describe the world he lives in? "How do people in the technology field think and behave?" and "Do they think at all?" as a friend once suggested after discussing the topic.

Another topic is raised again and again is why the most evolutionary steps concerning information technology happen more often in a small part of the United States, the Silicon Valley, than everywhere else. Why can't you have a Google, Amazon or Paypal spawning out of let's say Britain? This is an area that has been thoroughly analysed, but by offering some personal insights might contribute to the ongoing discussion. This can happen by shedding light into some not widely discussed subjects such as: "Are the societies willing to accept changes that will alter their production and distribution of wealth establishments?". Another one would be the role of hierarchy inside companies: "Are we willing to sacrifice hierarchical models for the benefit of innovation or accelerated wealth creation?". The answer is a negative one for the vast majority of the cases as some examples from the British IT landscape will be used to demonstrate it.

STRUCTURE

With the above in mind the book is divided into three intermingling parts. On the first there is the introduction and analysis of the main "roles" or archetypes of contemporary IT.

The second part is dedicated to day to day scenarios or incident in companies lives. Those are observed through the lens of the archetypes introduced on the first part.

Finally the third part consists of some semi-independent essays which examine concepts such as why so many people want to work for companies in the likes of Google, Facebook and Twitter, or why we do not have yet many Silicon Valleys. The arguments used are originating from the concepts of the first two parts, so the essays discuss some angles different than the ones more commonly brought up in blog posts or articles.

AUDIENCE

This book's target audience consists of two main categories. First one is people already engaged in the field of IT that would be interested in understanding more more about themselves and their colleagues or get an alternative perspective. The second category is people that their day to day life involves interacting with IT personel, something that will progressively occur more and more often in a period of time where "software is eating the world" and "every business is somehow a software business". The above category includes people who are tasked with allocating optimally candidates to companies or departments with managers, human resources specialists or recruiters being two examples.

This might be one of the few attempts to address the needs recruiter crowd. The occupation is both misunderstood and mistreated, sometimes conceptualised as necessary evil, a penalty someone has to pay for doing business. Having to manage a three way relationship involving the candidate, the target organisation and themselves there is the hope that the next pages might provide them with insights which could assist in reaching better conclusions faster. Similar is the case for typical HR. Keeping in mind that hiring decisions affect the well being of the candidates lived and the companies capability to operate, every contribution in these areas can have positive effect to people's lives.

Summarising this effort aims to be a know thyself guide for the IT people, a know thy-friends guide for the ones that interact with them. Or as Almost-Sun Tzu stated it in antiquity: *"If you know the people you work with and know yourself, you need not fear the result of a hundred projects. If you know yourself but not the people you work with, for every release to production you will also suffer a defeat. If you know neither the people you work with nor yourself, in every project you will suck."*

WHAT'S LEFT OUT

What was consciously left out was covering topics that have been already thoroughly investigated, debated and examined on the field, more or less since the 70s. The above include how to managing people in teams, how the ideal office environment should be for creative work, why employees should have state of the art equipment, the importance of getting into "the zone" or how to hire and grow a good team. There is a lot of material already available from authors who know these subjects better and have achieved far more than I will even be able to in this lifetime. Another reason is that people in our "ecosystem" have a binary approach towards reading: either they read a lot or they do not read at all. Paraphrasing the biblical "Whoever has ears to hear, let them hear", members of the former category have already been exposed to related material and members of the latter never read anything so there would be no added benefit for the either of those two categories from analysing the same subjects again, even more if there is material available from the 70s if not earlier.

I was trying to avoid two tendencies: the first is the "smoking is bad" category, saying the same thing with different wording every five years hoping that this time people will listen. The other one is the "author's first book" disease which involves inflating the book with content so that it will meet some length criteria. It is better to explore two or three subjects and leave the rest for a follow up or to existing works.

Thank you for reading this and let's start our journey!
Dimitry.

■

PART ONE

THE PEOPLE

PERSONALITY ARCHETYPES

I WILL USE MAINLY two sources to describe the people involved in the IT field: Robert Cringely's "archetypes" and Aldous Huxley's "caste divisions". A meld of these two concepts will be the main point of reference utilising the conceptualising power of the analogy and metaphor.

Robert Cringely, with his unique writing style, introduces in his taxonomy the "Commandos", "Infantry" and "Police" archetypes. This happens in his monumental book "Accidental Empires", on which he explains the mechanics of the computer industry as it had evolved at the time of writing the first version of "Empires" circa 1996. The archetypes are introduced in the twelfth chapter, titled "On the beach".[1] Cringely, looking back from mid 90s, described events that span through the 70s and 80s. These events are even more relevant today, almost two decades after the book was published as times change but people do not.

---

[1] "On the beach", available on-line: http://www.cringely.com/2013/03/18/accidental-empires-chapter-12-on-the-beach/

The second point of reference will be Huxley's casts division of populace in his dystopian novel "Brave new world". More specifically, I will utilise his references to "Alphas", "Betas" and "Gammas". "Deltas" and "Epsilons", the remaining two castes in Huxley's universe, also exist in modern workspaces but their limited mental capabilities would exclude them from doing any IT related work leaving them, as a result, out of our analysis. What makes Huxley's caste divisions very interesting and appealing is the extended descriptions of how a member of a caste understands their position in the world and how they comprehend and internalise day to day activities, life planning, or just random incidents. Another noteworthy theme is the patterns of behaviour towards members of the same or different casts: for example how a Gamma behaves towards another Gamma or towards an Alpha. These patterns provide a very useful tool to understand and describe the dynamics between roles.

For the purposes of our narrative, archetypes and caste divisions will be combined, suggesting that there is a one to one connection between them. Commandos are mapped to Alphas, Infantry to Betas and Police to Gammas. In this chapter, the mentality behind this mapping will be explained along with some comments. Later on, these concepts will be expanded along with related research and personal experiences, first by discussing each archetype in isolation. But first we will start with a fast revisit on Cringely's relevant chapter, serving as the starting point for our narration.

ARCHETYPES FROM "ACCIDENTAL EMPIRES"

As the narrative in "On the beach" goes, building a company is conceptualised as military operations in which an imaginary army will have to conquer enemy territory. This will happen in subsequent *waves* of assaults. The first wave consists of Commandos whose job is to *parachute behind enemy lines or quietly crawl ashore at night*. Their target is to *establish a beachhead* as soon as possible and that's what they have been trained for and are capable of doing. For achieving this, they need to *make creativity a destructive act* by solving all sorts of problems the moment they encounter them. They have to be creative, communicate with each other on an equal to equal basis, skilful, and - most important - cross-disciplined. What identifies Commandos is their need to operate outside of each one's comfort zone as they face problems that neither them nor maybe anybody else has encountered before; in short, live in chaos. In the context of IT companies, most of the times, but not always, this situation applies to the initial start-up or starting-up phase where the company is discovering its business model or it needs to create the infrastructure on which it will operate from scratch. Once some sort of "beachhead" is established, it is time for the second wave, that is the Infantry, to get into the picture.

The Infantry's function is to maintain the ground captured by Commandos and expand it. *While the Commandos make success possible, it is the Infantry that makes success happen.* These people are quite a different breed as they are mostly based on discipline and teamwork. They are very clever and in order to function they need orders or at least some sort of orientation. Orders given are respected and an Infantry member will do anything it can in its power to follow them. A key difference between Infantry and Commandos is that Infantry may face harsh or extremely difficult situations but definitely not the total chaos that Commandos is trained to encounter. Another difference is that the number of situations on which Infantry will need to act totally alone or make decisions is far smaller compared to Commandos. On the other hand, Infantry can solve problems as they arise and allow the operations to expand, one step at the time. Their process allows their targets to be reached incrementally in a stable and very often measurable way.

At the end, when there are no fierce battles and conflict, but there is *still a need for a military presence in the territory* (Cringely), we have the third wave which is essentially a Police force. The Police consists of people that are not extreme fighters, but can get through some difficult situations. In the cinematic war narrative, a Police force is tasked with occupying the land captured by the Infantry until the war is over. Their behaviour should be predictable and easy to scale. Being limited in their scope, their job is mostly to maintain the inherited state of affairs. In order to achieve this, they need to be very good at following orders and also behave according to specified patterns of behaviour.

An interesting observation from Cringely's analysis is that different people are more appropriate than others for different phases of the imaginary military operation or life-cycle of an actual IT company. With this in mind, some questions come up: What happens with Commandos after their specific wave function is completed? A possible answer could be that, until the end of the "war" or their "death", which projects to retirement for the IT working crowd, they prefer to remain as close to action as possible. In a business setting, once they finish their course, they delegate control to the next wave and then proceed deeper in the mainland. For example, other areas that the business needs the Commandos talent and capabilities. An almost identical approach can be followed from Infantry.

At the time the business has established itself, which is when the imaginary war is close to an end or already ended, almost only Police type employees are required. Based only on the time of their recruitment, it is impossible for them to have any memories or participation on how the organisation was in the past, when there was almost nothing in place, when the managerial structures and overall infrastructure had to be devised, implemented, and corrected. For Police members it is natural to assume that the way things are is the way things should be, so effort should be applied only for maintenance. It is possible for Police to assume that the first two waves never existed, with the exception of some employees that got hired early enough. Even then, these only a few individuals and their memories are distant.

After Police forces take over, some Infantry mentality might be in place for exceptions or opportunities that might arise, such as business expansion and, more or less, that's the final mix. Very few countries sustain a considerable number of real Commandos operational in time of peace. Similarly, businesses at their established stage do not want Commando people around. What happens, also mentioned from Cringely, is that Commandos either leave for the next business that needs them or they get pushed aside from management because they are considered no longer relevant - the current environment cannot contain them.

Summarising, Commandos create the status quo. Infantry stabilises and expands it. Police's role is to sustain and maintain it.

O BRAVE NEW WORLD

The second reference point comes from Huxley's masterpiece "Brave new world", set up in a near-future and very dystopian world which evolves around a tight caste system. A significant fact is that people in the "Brave new world" universe are genetically engineered in a laboratory where the caste on which they will belong to is predefined before birth. The makes of a person cannot be altered during the course of their lives.

On the top of the hierarchical pyramid sit the Alphas. They are not only the most intelligent ones who also engage actively with their assigned occupation or job function. Alphas are followed by Betas. They are also very intelligent and capable. Although Betas can comprehend a lot, they cannot "connect the dots" or generate new knowledge. Preconditioned by birth, Betas can understand as well as appreciate science only through its applications. They are not only unable but additionally unwilling to actively engage and produce science. In a similar fashion, Gammas find it difficult to do anything beyond following instructions and do not want to pursue further; following instructions makes them happy in their working lives.

In the centre of Huxley's narrative is the concept that each caste member's will and capability are essentially two sides of the same coin. A caste member does not wish to do anything outside their boundaries, nor they will ever try to. This also is true for the other way around, it would never succeed in crossing their boundaries so they would never wish to do so.

In Huxley's world, glorifying science and scientific method has elevated to religious status, a little bit above from the current levels that science is placed in the contemporary culture and workspaces. Gammas, for example, comprehend their relationship to scientific applications as an infinite list of different processes or prescriptions, somewhat a recipe approach: the better you follow the prescribed steps, the better the result that will come out of them.

With our "actors" identified above, we can describe and analyse them further. Then we will get to how castes and archetypes see and treat one another.

■

COMMANDO

PEOPLE BELONGING to the Commando archetype have a connection with their profession at a deeper level that often elevates to the level of identity: their profession is an integral part of their life, ingrained in who they are. While most people identify themselves around their profession, Commandos have a deeper connection than the usual. Consequently, they have a passion for all things related to their field but very rarely are they passionate for other fields, even ones neighbouring with their profession. This emotional attachment helps Commandos to produce better and high quality output. The same emotional attachment comes with "baggage" such as idealism, naiveté, excessive optimism and a wrong good will attitude. Especially in IT, there is also an increased reliance on scientific approach and methodologies to the point of neglecting other factors as a source of bias.

A Commando is usually talented with skills that cover a wide range of areas up to an adequate level. Some Commandos have reached mastery in some of these areas, with this happening more as a result of working on specific projects rather than being their original intention. Because Commandos wear many hats and are involved in different roles, their level of competence in each individual area ranges from good enough to very good; anything above that in a specific field is either occasional or accidental.

Based on experience, Commandos constitute approximately 5 to at most 10% of the workforce purely because the combination of personal traits, attitudes, and being in the appropriate industry is difficult to occur.

PORTRAIT

Outside work, a Commando is the kind of person that would experiment with learning coding a side-project using a new programming language that became recently hip within Internet circles. Or someone who follows a paradigm different from the mainstream just because it is intellectually interesting or will help give a broader perspective, for example LISP. Back in the 90s or in the 00s, it would be the person that would spend a free Saturday morning installing an arcane Linux distribution whose name would end in "-ux" or "-ware", a name that most people in the profession had never even heard of, on their home's desktop computer. Similarly, today a Commando might purchase a Raspberry Pi just for experimenting with the hardware. Alternatively, he/she might try to write an application on an Android device aiming to acquire a better understanding of how modern smartphones work under the surface or also get exposed to how the mobile application ecosystem is structured and why, or try to learn machine learning algorithms, or experiment with block chains and crypto-currencies. In order to engage with the activities described above, there is no need to have any relation with the day to day tasks assigned in the office.

EDUCATION – PROFESSIONAL DEVELOPMENT

A Commando prefers to try different approaches to problem solving, for which they are often criticized for continuously chasing the next "new thing". Personal development happens by visiting scheduled or unscheduled meet-ups, or by engaging in conventions with other similar minded people. Generally, they visit places where an exchange of ideas and know-how will take place, later on they will experiment on those either at their own time or at work in an attempt to learn or gain insights.

Essentially, Commandos can self-educate demonstrating intrinsic motivation since they want to learn and advance their disciple because of interest and love towards it.

This explains why many Commandos do not always follow a conventional academical path: being self-motivated and disciplined they can achieve the same or maybe better result without following the semester based pace set by a college professor or an institutional curriculum. Within an academic environment, they can fall into one of two extreme cases: either get far ahead of class and excel or not be able to maintain focus and drop out.

AT WORK

A Commando usually operates in one of the following two modes: moving as fast as possible and doing things right.

When there is no infrastructure in place in the initial phases of a project, a Commando will try to scrap a solution jumping between different domains, learning on the go if necessary. They can utilize short-cuts or even rely on half baked solutions knowing that they are "good enough" for the time being, acknowledging their limitations. Some hacking is a necessary sacrifice in order to ship a product on time or take advantage of a business opportunity.

Later though, in more stable environments, there is the desire to implement a choice that is technically correct from a given set even if this option leads to a disproportionate effort or changes to an existing system for its implementation. In the Commando mindset, for any given problem, the best tool should be used or the more appropriate methodology should be applied. As an example, for a greenfield web project the most appropriate programming language/framework combination should be used, say Node.js or Rails or Django, even if nobody in the team has any experience in any of those. Everyone should be able to learn as the project progresses. What is more important is to utilize the capabilities of the chosen platforms which will help to produce an elegant and proper solution.

ARGUING AND NEGOTIATING

Facing a disagreement, a Commando will first aim to detach the ego related or emotional parts of each argument. Commandos will try to prune out the rationally correct arguments of each side and examine if these can be validated or falsified. This will dictate which and whose opinion or approach should be adopted. It might be his/her personal opinion or might originate from an intern that has been in the company for two weeks or from a company veteran that has been there for the last ten years. As long as it is correct, nothing else should matter.

Comparing the Commando with the other two archetypes, arguing and negotiating are usually this archetype's Achilles heel. Projecting their own mental model of the world, Commandos treat discussions as an exercise that aims to discover some truths about their organization or the market, or alternatively as an attempt to discover the optimal solution for a particular problem that is being discussed. This is a slightly Quichotian approach that clashes with the reality of most organizations in which the vast majority of arguments has to do with people issues such as feelings and perceptions, as well as the process of negotiation.[1] The so called "human elements" of a negotiation or an argument are almost always more important than the actual facts or which opinion is correct. Commandos do not take the "human element" into account either because they are unaware of their importance or because they simply decide to bypass or suppress them believing that this is the correct approach. However, removing the "human element" from the equation can make Commandos slip from being technical high achievers.

AS A SUPERVISOR

It is more common to see a Commando as a supervisor or CTO in a start-up or in a small organization. This can result from a rapid expansion of a small team that they were originally leading or as a result of consequent internal promotions. In this case, most Commandos tend to follow two hiring principles: the "As that hire As that hire As" approach[2] and the "hiring the same people as you" pattern. The former because it is easy and natural for them to choose a candidate based on similar capabilities and world view, the latter because of the belief that similar people would be appropriate hires. Companies occasionally hire external Commando

---

[1]. For a more concrete reference see "Getting more" in bibliography.

[2]. Origin: Guy Kawasaki quoting Steve Jobs: "Steve Jobs has a saying that A players hire A players; B players hire C players; and C players hire D players. It doesn't take long to get to Z players. This trickle-down effect causes bozo explosions in companies.", http://www.goodreads.com/quotes/391717-steve-jobs-has-a-saying-that-a-players-hire-a

type people as supervisors or CTOs hoping that they will be able to single-handedly restructure a stagnated organization or department.

Stemming from their own personality traits, a Commando supervisor would provide extensive trust and autonomy in regards to decision making and would request very good results from his subordinates. The managerial style would be more transparent and supportive which is more appropriate for modern IT. On the bad side, there would probably be the assumption that everybody else shares the same approach and would make good use of the trust or the autonomy accordingly. This behaviour alienates people that require some structure around them or just want to be told what to do as it is the norm with the other two categories as we will describe in the following chapters.

∎

INFANTRY

PORTRAIT

The Infantry archetype would apply to a very capable and experienced person. This person would hold in-depth knowledge and possess a small number of capabilities at a high level of competence, something which is a deliberate and conscious decision. Within their working environment, Infantry would respect the existing state of affairs which they would be willing to game from time to time. Their attitude assures their co-workers they will accomplish the tasks assigned to them, and, ultimately, that allows Infantry to inspire trust in the people that they work with.

The limited skill-set in the number of capabilities is compensated for by a depth of knowledge which we rarely observe in the other two archetypes. For example, an Infantry person would be able to explain concepts such as how a database query is executed, while simultaneously identify how a specific version of the database system is going to handle the query compared with another version from the same vendor. Generally, Infantry have achieved mastery of their corresponding field or are on the path towards achieving that goal, justifying their salary to the penny.

Occasionally, the industry shifts between paradigms such as "going web" or "going mobile". Although an Infantry person is aware that such shifts occur, the decision to switch areas of expertise[1] is a result of deliberation and conscious thinking, related professional aspirations or derives from identifying a strong demand for talent in the future.

The Infantry's inclination is to "get the job done" and accomplish their assigned responsibilities that will help them advance both their careers and the objectives of their respective organizations. Though, as mentioned earlier on in the categorization chapter, their output is more of incremental nature: stable, predictable, measurable, balanced.

Based on experience, Infantry constitute approximately 10%-15% of the company's workforce. Compared with Commandos, they are more easy to find, not only because of their increased representation, but also because they can end up in a bigger number of companies.

EDUCATION – PROFESSIONAL DEVELOPMENT

Infantry prefers formal education which translates to colleges, universities, certifications, or alternatively extensive mentoring in the form of an apprenticeship. Additional skills can be acquired from places such as meet-ups, conventions and events. Essentially in surroundings where the aim is to be exposed to the learning material on the spot, usually in the form of something that resembles a

---

[1]. Or as the profession's slung would say, "ride another wave".

classroom such as a workshop. Some of the knowledge acquired should be ideally of use the next working day, with the seeds for deeper learning planted so that in due course it will bear fruit.

Learning material can be obtained from on-line resources and usually read at work during breaks or at home. The approach is in the semi-active - semi-passive zone: many Infantries would read blog posts for example or know the most prominent bloggers the same field as them. However, they would rarely take the initiative to contribute either by placing comments or, moreover, with something like starting a blog about their field themselves.

AT WORK

For the Infantry personality, day to day decisions have to do with finding the fine line between the current state of affairs and an optimal solution. With the latter being hard or possibly impossible to get to, things can only improve incrementally.

This infuses a strong element of pragmatism and the need to reach a compromise between potentially competing factors. An example of this approach from my experience is the following: Some years ago an organization needed to create a new web-based application. That organization was relying on Java-based frameworks which had eventually become out of touch with contemporary web development of the time. Some people had suggested that for the new web-based applications it would be best to stay with what the organization was already familiar with in order to maintain the capability to estimate milestones; a "the devil you know" approach. Some others, more partisan, asked to use "Ruby or Rails" or "Django" which were examples of the de-facto web development frameworks of the time. Our Infantry-style manager decided at the end to use "Grails", a niche framework self-described as: "A powerful Groovy-based web application framework for the JVM". Grails shares some Rails and Django concepts and is centered around the Java ecosystem with which the organization was familiar with. Definitely, some novel concepts had to be introduced and harnessed, though not in a sense that might jeopardize their capacity to deliver without causing major estimation errors. Developers would not suffer from regression shocks by having to learn too much; absorbing too many novel concepts in a short amount of time. The solution was removed from the ideal of using a modern, web-first application framework. On the other hand, it was now closer to that, thus making a step towards the right direction.

Company politics, although not always great, are treated as a fact of life which deserves its fair share of attention. Infantry people strategically choose not to challenge the status quo or to openly express something that would be against the consensus or the current groupthink.

Some criticism against Infantry would be that they tend to suggest solutions to problems that suffer Upton Sinclair's famous quote: "It is difficult to get a man to understand something when his salary depends upon his not understanding it.", where the constraining factor is an Infantry's chosen career path. Suppose that there is an organization which relies heavily on Oracle products and it decided to create a new application for a different market segment. What is the possibility of having a person who has been an Oracle database administrator for the last 15 years to objectively assess the situation and come up with an opinion in the following lines: "Oracle corporation recently started overcharging for licenses in order to balance out their shrinking market share caused by competing with new no-SQL offerings. Our new application would seem to be handled better by a

PostgreSQL database in the long run.", alternatively followed by: "... by introducing another database product we will minimize the dependency to a single vendor which can be used as negotiating leverage in the future". Would not there be an inclination from that person to favor an Oracle product for solution "X" or something similar which would fit better in the narrative their CV advertises? And at the same time increasing the compensation requirements from the next employer? The purpose of the example is not to suggest that each company's infrastructure should be balkanized using an amalgamation of products from different vendors. Instead, the example's purpose is to challenge how a person would react facing essentially a conflict of interest between their own career progression targets and the interests of the organization currently working for.

ARGUING AND NEGOTIATING

An Infantry person, as we described in the "Portrait" section, respects and accepts the current corporate hierarchy, the existing bureaucracy and established decision making process. There is also respect for the experience that a person has already accumulated either from having worked for a number of years for a specific organization or within one particular industry. This, coupled with a strong sense of technical expertise, allows them to see the full spectrum of an argument and conduct appropriate discussions. Compared to the other two archetypes, Infantries are those that can negotiate better than anyone else and this is one of the reasons that allow them to climb the corporate ladder faster: people within the organization find a person who not only has technical capability but can also listen, understand the background and where each person is coming from, suggesting solutions that have an acceptable risk factor.

AS A SUPERVISOR

Infantry supervisors can be employed by both small and large organizations alike. When many companies ask if they prefer to advance in a managerial or a technical career path, they have chosen the latter and educated themselves accordingly. Being people that value experience more than raw talent, they are eager to create a structure that promotes based on time on the job or in the industry which their company serves. This is one of the sources of "two years of J2EE" or "three years of web development in C#" job position advertisements. This perspective can blur the hiring or promoting process which might trigger the "Bs that hire Cs that hire Ds" circle of decay[2], in contrast with the "As that hire As that hire As" discussed in the Commando chapter.

An Infantry supervisor would like to conduct one on ones, experiments, learning workshops or training courses within the organization. Employees that want to advance can take a course, provided with time for self learning, or be allowed to attend a convention on company time and expenses. The above should be conducted without disrupting the existing state of affairs of the organization: if the CEO is against out of the office courses, there will probably not be a heated argument about out of office course benefits.

∎

---

[2]. Or as the original quoter would say "bozo explosion".

POLICE

PORTRAIT

Compared to the other two categories, Police personality-type people constitute the vast majority of the IT workforce. With a percentage around 80% of the total of the professionals in the field being a rough approximation. Similar ratios might possibly be the case in other industries as well.

A Police person can be best described as the guy/gal next door. What characterizes them is a passive relationship with their profession, an "it's just a job" approach. What drove them to the field was the field's career prospects and a narrative advocating that "this Information Technology thing is the occupation of the future where there will always be employment". For some specific cultures, members of specific castes are growing up knowing that they will end up becoming IT professionals without any choice of their own, which produces in turn a sizeable stream of Police people.

EDUCATION – PROFESSIONAL DEVELOPMENT

Stemming from the passive approach towards the profession, additional knowledge and novel concepts need to be infused to Police people from external entities. This happens because the incentives to learn or the intrinsic motivation are simply not there.

A curriculum taught in a classroom setting, be it in a college, university, or vocational training school, is strictly followed aiming to receive the degree or certificate at the end. This target will be achieved solely by following the tutor's instructions, doing the homework exercises and attending the classes. A Police person could sometimes request additional coursework for better grades, may ask some questions in the spirit of "what do I need to do to get a good mark?" or to clarify something not explained well enough. Occasional good marks achieved from time to time are treated as an added bonus.

This mentality is duly transferred over to the workplace. When there is the need to learn something substantial such as a new programming language or a framework utilizing a different paradigm, a Police person needs a setting that resembles a classroom. This can happen either through hiring an external tutor for courses in a conference room or booking a course in a training center. With getting things done on a day to day basis, the following two would be the first questions that come into mind: *"Can someone show me …"* and *"How do we do this here?"*.

Police's boundaries of knowledge and capability are those of the department of the company for which they are currently employed.

AT WORK

There are some attitudes in Police people that stem from their passive approach towards work: e.g., evaluation is being measured mostly by how someone follows established procedures as much as possible. When something out of the ordinary occurs, higher echelons of management have to be informed and consulted. Initiative should be kept to a minimum deferring as much responsibility as possible. Generally, there should be a rigid state which is considered normal; everything that diverts from that state needs to be regressed back, whether it is positive or negative.

This attitude has the side-effect that the only possible way for a Police person to improve his/her output is by working more: either extra hours or extra days on weekends. There is no other alternative because the Police person, even when in high managerial positions, would never initiate those processes that would eventually increase productivity or efficiency. Similarly, experience can only be acquired after passing some time in a specific position learning from occasional non-ordinary incidents that occur from time to time. Their comfort zone expands at a very slow pace.

Another area in which Police-type persons are more interested in improving, compared to the other archetypes, regards looking or talking appropriately as a token of professionalism. There is a general consensus that the more formally an IT person is dressed for the job, the less capable they are. This could explain why clueless consultants always wear suits; doesn't this help their professional opinion easier to accept?

ARGUING AND NEGOTIATING

When the overall state of the projects is immutable, different opinions or approaches can only result from personal relationships and different personality traits. If two people disagree on which source control system they should use for the next project, there is probably some subliminal conflict between them; maybe they tried to date and it did not go well or they do not like each other's religion or sports team. The answer to which version control system should be used is known beforehand: the one we already have. So the cause of an argument needs to be traced to something involving relationship between the people that disagree: egos, approaches, previous history, maybe some sort of discrimination. Similarly, whoever tries to rock the boat too much, should get back in line along with the rest of the Police people of the department or leave.[1]

Another predicator of whose opinion is more probable to be correct is hierarchy and number of years in the current business. Since knowledge can only come from experience (it terms of years), whoever is higher in the organizational chart or longer employed among equal peers is the one whose opinion should be right because this is the person that has worked more.

AS A SUPERVISOR

As discussed above, the purpose of the Police personality is to ensure stability mostly by adherence to the corporate processes and practices or preserving the way things were historically conducted. When the need comes to solve a hard problem or an unexpected situation, the solution is to ask the personnel to work

---

[1]. The department, the company, or even the planet.

more or hire more people if necessary.

Similarly, training and education programs aim at training people on how things are currently manifested in the current department with the current choices. The educational system should be education about the system. One on ones, career progression discussions or other managerial tasks are treated as a luxury or nice to haves, or something that should be avoided as much as possible.

Eventually the Police type supervisor ends up living in a world at work has to do mainly with adhering to existing processes and practices where there are very few ways to distinguish the employees such as how pleasant they are to him or the perception of how hard, but never how smart, they work. Sooner or later a Police-type supervisor will make the mistake of hiring people that are less capable than himself. They will inevitably do the same resulting in a progressive decline of the capability of the organisation.[2] This, especially in the IT sector, can accelerate faster than in other industries due to the inherent velocity of change within the sector.

As supervisors, Police people are in general ideal for well established industries or occupations where stability and predictability is preferred. It is important that there is no immediate paradigm shift looming over the horizon. Police supervisors can also serve many IT businesses: companies that have long term contracts that support very specific organizational structures on the client side, companies whose market status is protected by an artificial monopoly, or where IT is a very small part of an organization and keeping it stable reduces the overall managerial workload.

---

[2] "Cs that hire Ds that hire Es", continuation of the "bozo" explosion from the Steve Jobs quote on Commandos chapter.

KICKING AROUND

The author of one of the first books on managing IT, "Peopleware"[3], while discussing the cookie-cutter management style in a formal meeting of professionals in London heard the following summarisation of the assembly line approach on management, the following statement: "**Management is kicking ass**". For many Police type companies, the manager's role can be reduced to that of a delicate polite bottom kicker. The emphasis is on the bottom kicker part of course.

The above analogy, even if pessimistic, summarizes the world view of most Police style / Gamma managers one will ever meet. Some of them might prefer to be gentle trying get a buy-in or engagement from their reporters. They might buy them a coffee and give a long lecture on how things cannot change. They might explain that what was going on in the previous company someone worked for or what was taught in that college with that prestigious name cannot apply here.[4] Some others might threaten with bad performance reviews if people do not work all day in the office, or something aggressive. There are many alternatives on how to deliver the message and how to sugar-coat the pill; the essence of the message though will always be the same: some sort of a bottom is receiving some sort of a kick.

∎

---

[3]. See bibliography for book's details.

[4]. In this industry/company/vertical/specific clientele.

HOW THEY SEE EACH OTHER

"I want to know what passion is. I want to feel something strongly."
– Aldous Huxley, Brave New World

WHILE THE PREVIOUS CHAPTERS gravitated more towards "Accidental Empires", this one evolves more around "Brave new world"'s universe. A main concept there is that members of each specific caste conceptualise themselves and their fellow members of the same caste as the only who are normal, those that got it right as it should be. The ones belonging to lower castes are treated as less capable or too distracted and lazy. Similarly, those belonging to higher castes are treated as too engaged in their jobs, taking things to the extreme, letting life pass by without enjoying it. Although behaviours are not as harsh as in Brave New World's dystopia, the analogy can be used for our archetypes.[1]

---

[1]. Not forgetting that the assignment of people to archetypes or castes is a generalisation, so not everyone is something 100%. Because of this there cannot be a caste system similar to that in Huxley's universe in the real world.

In order to emphasise the Huxley element the castes will be referenced as Alphas, Betas, and Gammas, with the direct projection of Alphas to Commandos, Betas to Infantries, Gammas to Police.

Expanding on these analogies centred around Huxley's approach, most Alphas (Commandos) and to some extent Betas (Infantry) are in their profession because this is what they wanted to do: each person for a variety of reasons chose to do IT among different occupations. Most Gammas on the other hand are there because they had to or were told to do so. Mixing them in the same organisation has ramifications such as them having conflicting opinions. Most of the time conflict or other effects are triggered subconsciously.

With a member of each caste seeing normality in itself and its peers, we will explore their attitude towards others. Reversing the usual order, we will begin with Gammas/Police's perspective and move from there to Alphas/Commandos.

THE GAMMA/POLICE PERSPECTIVE

Gammas treat the workspace as a necessary evil part of life, an inevitability pretty much on the same level as death and taxes. This means that the workplace might be nice or tolerable, which, when it happens is more than welcome, but at the end of the day it doesn't matter. At the end of the day being there is the sacrifice that has to be made so that the rest of life can be enjoyed.

Through this lens the other two archetypes are viewed as not only having a different agenda or different orientation, but moreover an at least incomprehensible behaviour. In one phrase they have got the whole thing wrong: instead of trying to enjoy life as much as possible they seem to be too concerned about what happens at work. With Betas there seems to be some sort of reasoning and they can somehow be comprehended, Alphas simply do not make any sense.

Betas might be oriented towards pursuing a career, be in need of a promotion, lured by the prestige of being called a professional. It is possible that they just happen to like what they are doing a little bit more than usual - nobody is perfect after all. Whatever might be the case, things do not get out of proportion confining them to normal socially acceptable limits.

Alphas, probably within the same lines, seem to have taken an extreme path. They seem to be talking about their field as if it is a bit more important than it should be. They seem to spend much time on reading things on the Internet such as the latest trends in their field of interest or studying alternative approaches on everything under the sun. They cheat themselves into believing that what somebody wrote on a blog-post is real so much that they would like to apply that in the workplace preferably by tomorrow, risking the stability of the business. If alas they actually manage to do so, Gammas might need to readjust to a radically new situation that will push them way out of their comfort zone, distracting them from other activities that really matter to them along the way.

BETA/INFANTRY PERSPECTIVE

Betas perspective is the most interesting of all three which stems from being positioned in the middle of the taxonomy from where they can empathise and associate with both other castes while at the same time maintaining an individual perspective and motivation. Because of this empathy, a Beta's approach is the most mild one as it can include elements of acceptance and understanding, being more inclusive than the other two.

For a Beta, Gammas can be those that do not care that much or just do not possess motivation or necessity to perform: people that ended up in the wrong career trajectory or treat their profession for what it is for most people, a job. Maybe they need some additional incentives or more specific instructions to get things done, but generally they are fine. Their presence in an organisation ensures a smoother career progression because they are easier to compete with, making a Beta's life easier.

Alphas also have a point as they get overenthusiastic and fascinated by the current trends wanting to experiment with them. Their opinions though should be taken with a pinch of salt as their in many cases radical approach might disrupt or even damage the existing infrastructure or capability of the team to deliver. Maybe they will change behaviour when they start getting interested in other aspects of life such as starting a family or when they discover a more engaging activity such as a hobby.

Alphas do not pose that much of a competition as their partisan approach usually scares off management. When management wants stability, which is most of the time, it will ask a professional which is almost always a Beta. An Alpha's enthusiasm about their field makes them also less receptive to needs of other parts of the business. Alphas can also function as trailblazers showing where the industry will navigate in the following years. Observing them is a better way to spot trends early on. For those two reasons, in the long run, Alpha's presence can be only beneficial.

ALPHA/COMMANDO PERSPECTIVE

As a reverse reflection of Gammas' perspective, Alphas can empathise with Betas and accept them, while this does not happen so much with the Gammas.

Betas can be viewed as "Broken Angels", angels who at some point in time lost their wings or were born with broken ones. They could have been essentially the same but somehow along the line they got diffused or cast down. Alternatively, they choose of a different path which might seem somehow odd to the Alpha's eyes but accepted and respected.

As Gammas could think that Alphas push it too far, similarly Gammas are too disengaged or conservative in Alphas' eyes. Gammas' behaviour might a result of not having enough capability or talent, or from being positioned in the wrong industry. In either case the questions remain the same: why don't they try harder or why don't they change industries? Also, for a number of companies: What gets them promoted, is it something related to politics, counting years on the job?

REVISITING HUXLEY'S NARRATIVE

Huxley's narrative provides interesting insights on how castes comprehend each other. In his universe Gammas are assigned prescribed repetitive procedural tasks that are inherently boring. In order to cure the boredom they are rewarded with amusements and other activities after the end of their shift. One of these is the overuse of drugs. There is one scene in the book where people are handled "soma", the euphoric substance of "Brave new world", just after finishing their shift in a factory. One could see an eerie resemblance with a modern metropolis, looking at people getting obsessed with their cell phones the moment they get out of the office. For many of them when one more day of writing politically correct compliant jargon-speak emails or answering phone calls based on a script has come to an end, it is time to get distracted with something that would carry them along to the next same day.

Betas in Huxley's world enjoy more autonomy and perspective but always within the boundaries of the system they serve - either their company or society in general. They have access to more challenging and difficult to comprehend material while being able to make their own decisions and impose them on Gammas or other more junior Betas. Maybe this is the reason that they do not rely so much on drug usage as the Gammas. The material to which they are exposed to has been censored in advance so that it is not possible to divert from what is accepted as cultural norm in "Brave New World"'s society. Generally, they live happily.

Alphas are entitled to a wider perspective and the ability to peek outside the box. This allows them the freedom to be exposed to material that is forbidden to the rest of society, see the "whole picture" and direct trends. Compared with the other castes, they are mostly engaged with the responsibilities which keep them active. Being in this situation removes their reliance on distractions or drugs which makes them the only ones that can allow themselves to have feelings such as sadness.

WHOSE OPINION WINS AN ARGUMENT

There is no deterministic formula but there is a strong indication that the result is influenced by the mentality of the company, its current life-cycle stage, the perspective of management, and maybe chance. Specifically, the stages in a company's life and relations to archetypes are the topic of the next chapter.

■

PART TWO

GAMES PEOPLE PLAY

COMPANIES

HAVING IDENTIFIED the Archetypes individually, it is possible to zoom out and conduct the same analysis for entire organisations such as companies. Although there is an analysis on Accidental Empires, a subsequent approach seems more appropriate, the one of Peter Thiel on his "Zero to One".[1] The numerical system identifies three almost distinct stages:

Zero to One: This is the initial stage of a company which starts with nothing (zero) and tries to produce something (one). This stage involves a lot of experimentation, pivots, changes in the suggested business model and direction. The stage ends when things start becoming concrete and the organisation has decided that from now on it will follow a certain trajectory. These activities, getting back to chapter one, are related to the establishment of the "beachhead".

---

1. The direct mapping would be first, second, and third wave which is how Cringely in Accidental Empires approaches it. The approaches are very similar but Peter Thiel's seems a little bit closer to what is being described and is also simpler. It is also interesting to triangulate with an additional point of reference.

One to Ten: The company's business model has been more or less validated and established while, in this process, some infrastructure has been set up and is operational. The biggest by-product of the previous stage is that the company has orientation and identity. In this stage, the emphasis is in streamlining the previous successes while also scaling them up. "One" needs to be applied to a wider audience or market segment and become "Ten".

Ten to hundred: In this stage things are more certain, while expanding from the previous stage, many lessons have been learned, lots of wisdom has been gathered and the company has now formed its "recipe" for success. Now, this recipe needs to be applied as much as possible: it is when companies become global or start entering many similar markets. There is some room for adjustment but the need for it is far smaller, especially compared with the two previous stages. The company is mostly cloning itself here.

After that stage, usually two things can happen[2]:

Hundred to Zero - Death: Because the company is too busy cloning itself, at some point it reaches its natural limits either because it totally serves its market segment or because its current approach has reached its peak. From then on, the company's management and structure are interested more in maintaining the existing status, perhaps with some minor cosmetic adjustments. The death at this point can come from either a disruptor or from irrelevance. Companies at this size are unable to counter disruptors precisely because they have become too big to manoeuvre or too self-absorbed. Alternatively, they might slip to irrelevance, such as Blockbuster renting DVDs while the world has become digital.

---

[2]. This is an expansion devised for this chapter so it does not originate from "Zero to One" nor "Accidental Empires".

Hundred to Zero - Rebirth: A very rare change of direction historically is when a company uses the experience accumulated as well as its cash reserves to reinvent itself and adjust to new market conditions. The most well-known but not the only example is Steve Job's return to Apple in the late 90s.

ARCHETYPES APPROPRIATE FOR DISTINCT COMPANY STAGES

While there is not a direct one-to-one relationship, describing the stages above and considering the archetypes, it would appear that a company in its "Zero to One" stage would be better served by Commandos, "One to Ten" by Infantry and the rest by Police.

In the first stage, there is too much uncertainty and the IT department is usually small, while having to make many decisions in diverse number of areas that demand attention. It could be application development, architecture, third party integrations, deployment management, security, systems administration, user experience design, and probably many others. Apart from the above, it is very common to have to conduct some so called "pivots" or encounter setbacks forcing many of these decisions to be revisited.

The above paints a picture of a landscape more friendly to Commandos. Whoever is engaged in these stages needs to be able to adapt, learn new skills on the go or expand their existing ones. There also needs to be high communication bandwidth among employees and their management. The corporate environment in that stage can easily become chaotic, resulting in a place where few rules of traditional corporate governance apply.

In the "One to Ten" stage, employees need to stabilise and manage the aftermath of the previous stage: the user interface might be inconsistent or use wording that makes it very difficult to translate to other languages, the database architecture cannot scale further and needs to be reconsidered, that code module needs to be expanded to accommodate a number of different businesses rules, or checkout procedure needs to include promotions and discounts.

Compared with a company in the "Zero to One" stage, let's consider the case when the database infrastructure needs to expand from a single MySQL node to a cluster of two but in a way that will be easy to scale up to ten. In our example, the person responsible for this has a boundary which was not there before: the most important is the fact that it is established that the database system is MySQL probably with a known number of applications interacting with it, containing a specific database schema. There is a well defined situation that needs to be managed. Some things might have to be adjusted or disrupted in the process but no high impact decisions are to be made such as dropping the MySQL altogether and rewriting all the application code that interacts with data, say, in Oracle.

Another factor is that, in some cases, things need to change gradually within the course of months or maybe years; an exercise that requires persistence and discipline. An example of this could be a change in the user interface that requires the use of a different theme including colour for company branding purposes. Because users are already using the applications and should not be disrupted by facing a completely different user interface overnight, a plan needs to be in place for changing a few elements at a time and by a small degree so that the changes will easily be digested and accepted. Over the course of time, the theme will reach the desired state, while looking as decent as possible in the intermediate stages. In the first wave phase someone would rewrite all the necessary modules and just "drop" the changes as they happen. This is the reason why early stage companies often have a different layout and theme in their home page and a different one once users log in.

SKIPPING STAGES, A HISTORIC PERSPECTIVE

This section refers to established companies that somehow skipped the first stages. For them, IT is either an afterthought, in theory they could work without it, or acts to support the organisation; IT is not a first class citizen. In order to understand corporate structuring of these companies, it helps to remember or imagine how the world of business used to be before the arrival of the personal computer and when it started being introduced.

Traditional businesses and organisations, say General Motors or government agencies, envisioned early on how information technology could make them more efficient and productive in their core functions. IT acts as a productivity multiplier and also as the ultimate facilitator. From this aspect, no matter how important, IT is always destined to be a servant. Such environments foster Police/Gamma type employees: What is really important happens somewhere else and they are here to offer support.

In the old days, a manager would dictate a memo or a letter to a typist which would then be faxed or photocopied and distributed. A modern manager would type it or, in some cases, still dictate what would become an email which then propagates through the corporate network via an email server. In this paradigm, infrastructure and the personnel supporting it have the same function and influence to the organisation as that of the secretary plus that of the person who fixes the photocopier or the fax machine and does the phone line maintenance combined.

By adopting this approach, IT is serving the business with a small impact on existing power structures or established decision making processes. A very useful and insightful cliché that was traditionally used when something becomes mechanised was usually that automation "... allows people to work with the information instead of gathering data...", essentially doing the same thing but smaller, cheaper, or faster. What does not change is who decides what should be done and how, the internal processes and who holds authority. An observation is that in many traditional organisations there is an organisational chart with a CTO role reporting theoretically straight to the CEO. In practice though, a CTO reports to basically everyone else who holds a "C" role or maybe not even that. In some places, where things fail or someone cannot do their job, the first attempt is to somehow try to blame IT.

Another concept that originates from the traditional business world is the tendency to try to make information technology related professions similar to existing traditional ones. Should not there be a professional body that grants licenses as it happens with doctors, civil engineers and also gardeners? How do we know that you can use a technology without being certified by its vendor or an independent institution? If configuring an email server is a job for a systems administrator then why should a developer ever be allowed near it? Shouldn't someone re-sit the scrum exams every two years? When are these people going to become just like rest of us?

OTHER TOPICS ABOUT COMPANIES AND ARCHETYPES

A NOTE ON THE PIONEERS, SETTLERS, TOWN PLANNERS APPROACH

This is an alternative model suggested at around 2005-06 by Simon Wardley, who is inspired, similarly to this book, by Cringely's distinction. On a first reading, it seems that Wardley gives credit and love to every member of his taxonomy while in this publication there is some disdain towards the Police category. Comparing with the thesis of this book, there seems to be something going wrong: why does one author seem to approve of everybody while another[3] seems to hold some grudge against Police/Gammas?

Reading of a post[4] with the definitions, the magic word in Simon Wardley is "innovation": his Pioneers, as well as his Settlers, and also his Town planners innovate in different areas with different targets. Nevertheless, they innovate or add value each in their own way. Comparing with the approach of IT Archetypes, Pioneers and Settlers could be mapped to Commandos/Alphas, Settlers and Town planners to Infantry/Betas, yet there is no one that maps to Police/Gammas. Maybe, from his perspective, these people are unnecessary or should not participate in the work force, or from where he sits, he does not have to encounter them.

COMMENTS ON DIVERSITY AND INCLUSIVENESS

The specific subject has become popular recently so it is beneficial to investigate it with regards to our taxonomy. After his personal research on the subject,

---

[3]. Definitely me, perhaps also Cringely.

[4]. http://blog.gardeviance.org/2015/03/on-pioneers-settlers-town-planners-and.html

Stuart Diamond in "Getting More" summarises: *"The biggest cause of growth in the U.S. gross national product since the end of World War II has been new technology. New technology has been largely developed by innovators and innovators are different. They represent change. They represent a level of discomfort as new things are tried and instituted"*. Specifically to the internal structuring of a company: *"if someone says to me 'We are different from each other', I am going to say 'Great! We are going to make money!' Homogeneity is not as profitable as Differences. I like to say 'get some people who disagree with us so that we can make more money'"*

Zero to One companies want to maintain a good mix of talents and capabilities because they need to be strong in many areas while the emphasis might shift from time to time based on the needs of the company. The people they want to attract need to have a wide spectrum of capabilities, each with their own strengths and weaknesses. The way the accumulation of those will behave will determine the shape of the company. It is acceptable to have people from different backgrounds maintaining their capabilities and orientation working together.

One to Ten companies are even more oriented towards inclusiveness. There is an orientation and elements of business culture in place where an individual comes to contribute with his/her own experiences and opinion towards the goal, influencing but not determining the outcome. It is common when having to complete a new task to ask questions such as "Could we do it differently?", "How did you manage that in your previous company?", "Is there a better way to...?".

Ten to Hundred companies do not really want a mix of talents as they aim to create a mono-culture. There, each employee is measured against how he conforms to the company's established norms and way of doing things. They really do not want to diversify at all. Though, because the term is popular, usually the following pattern of behaviour is utilised: the companies hire people with different racial, national, religious or other backgrounds who then have to get dressed, talk, behave the same way or approach each business situation the same way and then they call this diversity. They project the image of a company that "has offices all over the world" or has "people from 999 countries", but it looks like a rewrite of the words of Tacitus: "where they make a wasteland, they call it peace", here *"where they hire people from different countries/races/genders, they call it diversity"*.

A TRANSACTIONAL ANALYSIS PERSPECTIVE

Somehow similar conclusions can be derived from applying transactional analysis[5] to stages of companies. In transactional analysis, people conduct interactions within one of three potential states: as an adult, as a child or as a parent. When a child interacts with another child we have states of "play" such as exploration, discovery, creativity. When two adults interact, we have clear communication based on facts, opinions, understanding, a one-to-one conversation. A different state is when an adult becomes a parent and communicates with a child, or another adult that adopts the behaviour of a child. There, the parent is either nurturing (*"I am asking you to do as I say for your own good"*) or critical (*"do as I say or else punishment"*). Similarly the person behaving as a child can be either adaptive (*"yes"* - but without understanding why) or rebellious (*"no"* - but again without knowing why).

---

[5]. An introductory paper is available here: http://www.carolsolomonphd.com/web_pdfs/Transact.pdf also in bibliography.

With a crash course on transactional analysis projecting to the company taxonomy, in the first "Zero to One" stage, the playful behaviours have to be necessary or dominant in order to create and discover something new. Afterwards, the company becomes a business or enters its adulthood where adult behaviours are more prevalent. The company has discovered which game it is going to play in the previous phase and now it needs to follow some rules and excel at it. In the Ten to Hundred phase, some adults are supposed to know how things should be and employees acting as children should trust them and follow their lead.

The concept of killing childhood or play-states and how it is conducted is the subject of the next chapter, where its mechanics' consequences are discussed from an archetype perspective.

∎

ONE TO TEN GENTRIFICATION

> "The constant issue is, what do you do with your heroes when you're finished with them? Norse mythology (and also the Greeks, I think) had a very clear sense of what you do with them: The heroes always have to die. The standard pattern for a heroic profile is that you fight in your great battle, and you succeed, and then shortly thereafter you go off to another battle, or very often to another land, and there you are betrayed or you die or you disappear from knowing and it's assumed that you've died. In each case, the hero is off-loaded. Those guys don't stick around — you don't keep them."
> – Richard K. Morgan[1]

ONE OF THE MOST intense transitions in a company's life can be the one from the initial start-up phase to the next one, that of steady growth. This happens because the capabilities and the approach required from its people are radically different than before as there is a shift towards stability which becomes progressively more important. The question in this case is what should happen to the existing employees who have a different approach and orientation. Similar questions

---

[1]. Clarke's world, issue 24, September 2008. Online: http://clarkesworldmagazine.com/morgan_interview/

have to be answered on a smaller scale within larger organisations that assemble innovation teams once they succeed in their mission.

No matter how obvious or inevitable this process seems, how much material is available on-line or in print describing it, or how much it is unanimously expected to happen, it is never a pleasant situation to participate in. Moreover for the people standing at the Commando side of the fence, as they are the ones to be ousted.

CONGRATULATIONS YOU ARE FIRED[2]

One option is to politely communicate that current employee's services are no longer required and that they need to move on to something else outside of the organisation they built. "Congratulations" are awarded because the people involved succeeded in achieving something very difficult: Got started when the company was on a concept stage, raised it to start-up and then transformed it to a functional business. Alternatively, they have completed an ultra difficult project that the rest of the company would have never done, or managed to turn around a company losing market share or even flirting with bankruptcy.

The very moment this stage is reached, the same people that placed the organisation on its current state are now considered a threat to its further survival. Their experimental forward-pushing nature will at some point result in conflict between the existing product strategy which now needs to be expanded and scaled. By no means should it be altered or tweaked into something different. How long will it take until they will want to experiment more, think of something else or de-

---

[2]. Could not trace the origin of the quote, but it seems to have reached the status of a "term" in start-up literature.

cide to tackle another different endeavour altogether? Will they push the company's offerings too much into the future so that nobody will be able to understand them and purchase them?

This is exactly what needs to happen up until the "congratulations" point where the business needed to experiment, pivot, or generally find its way among a multiplicity of options. Once this is achieved, a different skill set altogether is necessary hence the "fired" part comes in. In some cases, it can happen nicely by exercising stock options, bonuses. In others in a more pushy way.

ORGANISATIONAL STABILISATION

Another approach to signal that things have changed is to start changing the organisational structure in such a way that becomes unbearable to current employees. When this happens, employees either have to swallow their pride and accept a situation that they are not fit for or eventually leave. This is usually achieved through the hiring process. Before the "congratulations" moment, management is hiring people with a mentality similar to the existing one, where newcomers will work alongside the current employees. In the stabilisation phase, this trend can be disrupted in two ways: either by purposefully diluting the mix of existing employees or by hiring managers who are fit to manage the company as it should be in its next stage.

Dilution is facilitated by consciously hiring Betas or Gammas either as peers or for similar positions. It can progress smoothly as the company expands or while replacing employees that for some reason had to leave the company. Some of the newcomers might adapt to the existing Commando mentality, some might be unable to and leave early. In either case, as this process progresses, at some point the existing employees will either become a minority or they might collectively get the message and start leaving the company in large numbers.

An alternative approach is a top-bottom one. Management can appoint as head of department a person that has "successful X years or experience" in the sector who used to work for an already established organisation. That person will bring along all the corporate baggage that would help him manage effectively according to his belief system, usually tools of bureaucratic control and reporting. Existing employees soon find themselves on top of their tasks having to write a 15 minute report of what they did that week every Friday, a report which is never read or feeding every detail of what they are doing to a corporate resource planning tool such as Jira or its siblings. It will not take long before they realise that they are valued based on how good reporters or yes-men they have become while just some months before they were judged by the output of their work.

Both of the cases above yield the same result: Alphas will be moving away or being side-lined while replacements better suited to the current management will take their place.

JONATHAN'S STORY OF MANAGERIAL STABILISATION

In one organisation I used to work for there was Jonathan, a guy very interested into Internet marketing, search engine optimisation, Google Adwords and similar analytics tools. Being in his mid to late twenties and a digital native always helped. Not only he was bright but he knew these concepts first hand as he had managed some small businesses of his own as well as those of his wealthy relatives. The hero of our story had his share of issues: he was pushing sometimes too fast, he did not respect hierarchy, especially some old suits from the mother company who wanted to have the last word on stuff, as well as the illusion of control by suggesting trivial tweaks, just to have their input in the end result. Jonathan might also occasionally over-rely on his own judgement. However you saw it, his advantages overshadowed all potential disadvantages that he might have and it was nice to work with him.

As the department was doing well and the company was expanding, everybody thought that an intern or an out-of-university recruit would join under Jonathan, absorbing the ways he did his magic and replicating it. Together they might be able to be more responsive to upper management and have the whole operation more smoothly. Instead of that, we got Mark. Mark was slightly obese, slow as a person, quite older than Jonathan, with a CV that was decent but definitely not impressive. The first thing that distinguished him from the other employees was the speed with which he was grabbing the doughnuts that the head of an another department was purchasing as a treat every other Friday[3], or the left-overs from the sandwiches that the management team was leaving for the plebs to consume after their quarterly meeting.

While Mark could not add any significant value, he was placed directly above Jonathan as the manager of his department and subsequent hires would report to him directly. His knowledge of the industry or the tool chain was not significant. His main contribution was to slow down Jonathan significantly, asking him random details or micro-managing him by adding a sign-off layer to every semi-important decision. By now, the reader would be able to guess how this story ended: Jonathan left after three months for a small company which offered a good equity package, two replacements were hired to expand what he had already build but

---

[3]. We are in Britain, please no doughnuts, we have mini-scones or other better things...

not actually change it a lot. Mark kept the suits happy by keeping them in the loop, having lots of time in his hands since he was not contributing considerably. Eventually the management found out that he was pretty useless, so instead of firing him he left on his own adding another decent but not superb entry to his CV.

RE-LEARNING

Re-learning is the most smooth, honourable, while unfortunately at the same time rare option. Current employees are invited to lead the transition towards the next stage of the company being provided with assistance from management and the resources to do so. They are asked to transform themselves and become what would have been their replacement. This approach is easier to progress more smoothly towards this direction if the existing employees are aligned with the mission of the company, interested in influencing the industry in which it operates, or just want to extend their time of employment within the same company without having to look for a job.

The re-learning approach can lead to great results in case the current employees are willing to let go of their current mentality. The changes can also be introduced as an another challenge that will add new skills to the existing employees helping them expand beyond their traditional domains.

DIFFERENT ASSIGNMENTS

An approach that happens more in theory than in practice has to do with optimising talent allocation: let current segments of the organisation evolve more gradually, and keep Alphas/Commandos for areas that still require their approach. It can be that a product has established Web presence and now there needs to be a mobile offering, or that because of the product's or service's success, new challenges have risen in scaling either in systems administration or development. Aligned with the quote on the beginning of the chapter, it is the *"another distant battle"* approach which our heroes have to fight.

The difficulties with this approach have to do with having two different managerial approaches in parallel within the same organisation: one serving rapid expansion and one for stable growth, which leads to managing completely different people. In addition, the company must decide on how these two worlds should communicate with each other and how priorities are set. Last but not least, after some time the new number of new fronts "ends", what should happen then?

WHAT IS LOST WHEN GENTRIFICATION IS OVER

The most important casualty of these gentrifications is creativity and the capability to introduce novel solutions to the organisation's problems. As the number of people that can think out of the box becomes smaller, even the ones that can do will be a silenced minority with their opinion never able to raise through the managerial layers. As a side-effect, the second casualty is the ability to adjust fast to a shifting marketplace falling behind or to identify opportunities early on. An organisation in this stage will need to hire expensive external consultants or firms to uncover and explain what previously was in plain sight.

An example story with an interesting twist that summarises this shift comes from what happened in NASA's Jet Propulsion laboratory[4]. In the early 90s, the people that were responsible for the marvels of the 60s and 70s had started to re-

---

[4]. "Play: How it Shapes the Brain, Opens the Imagination, and Invigorates the Soul", Stuart Brown M.D., Christopher Vaughan. Did not add the title to Bibliography since only the specific incidents are referenced.

tire. Most of them were from a non-academic background, essentially self-taught. Their replacements had Ph.D. titles from prestigious universities. Although the younger academics were perfect on paper, they were unable to match the problem solving capabilities of their seniors, leaving the laboratory unable to fulfil its purpose.

"My company does not dispatch rockets to the Moon, or does not do robotics for the ISS", was the excuse that many would utilise justifying what they did to their companies, though here comes the story's twist. NASA's people started asking around when they got a response from Nate Jones, a man who was running a machine shop specialising in tires for Formula One and other similar racing competitions. Nate was facing exactly the same situation as the people he was hiring for his company were not as good in problem solving as their self-taught previous employees. After interviewing and juxtaposing the two generations of engineers, he found out that the previous generation of self taught ones were used to *"play with their hands as they were growing older, were able to 'see solutions' that those who hadn't worked with their hands could not"*. The Formula One company reminds far more a modern knowledge-based company in roles not only related to engineering but also in other disciplines, even if we rule out NASA's laboratory as exotic. Similarly, the description of old guards that got replaced fits a lot with the Alpha or Commando archetypes, while their replacements as the Beta or Infantry.

Essentially, what is being relinquished is the ability to "play". The only way to reverse this course is by hiring Steve Jobs back, this though happens only once since there are very few people that are capable of turning things around and also available to do so at a time of need.

■

POLICEMEN KILLING MACHINE

AS THE PREVIOUS CHAPTER, "One to Ten gentrification", was about how Commandos "die", which is how they are removed from the organisations they built, this chapter is about how Police employees die, that is how they lose their jobs from the organisations they support.

There are two ways for Police personnel to be terminated: their organisation dies, or their organisation kills them by sending them and their projects to an Elephant's graveyard for dead IT.

END OF THE STORY

The first possibility is that Police's employment ends as a Police style organisation starts taking the path that will gradually lead to irrelevance. At some point, their company's targeted market segment will be better served by the competition. As the company's market share drops, continuing its operations will eventually no longer be feasible.

In that case, Police people's employment terminates either as the organisation closes shop or after being a sale or merge with an another corporate entity. Subsequent restructuring of the company will make their current position redundant.

THE STUPEFY/OUTSOURCE/AUTOMATE KILLING MACHINE

Another pattern that is more common for big corporations that have managed to survive for prolonged periods of time and paradigm shifts in the industry is the following which is very intelligent in the results that it achieves. Essentially it involves moving the project to an Elephant's graveyard for IT projects[1] in one of the many locations around the world.

The first step has to do with stupefying the operations of a specific organisation structure as much as humanly possible. There will still be a need for human supervision and interaction, but Police employees should be forced to act more as "human robots" within their job role. The outcome of this exercise is a department that has very concrete boundaries and specific inputs and outputs. It is then easy to comprehend and manage and that smooths the subsequent outsourcing.

Once the initial step is finalised, then follows a time of intense documentation and similar activities such as process mapping, whose target might be presented to the participants as an optimisation exercise but its actual aim is to make it as easy as possible to explain to an external entity how things are done.

The intermediate step is to change nothing internally on the department in

---

[1]. Definition: "An elephants' graveyard is a place where older elephants instinctively direct themselves when they reach a certain age. They then die there alone, far from the group.". It is a myth - such places do not exist, but it has been rooted in popular culture.

question apart from its location and its personnel. A popular outsourcing target used to be India but due to the economic development of the country and the need to serve the domestic audience, other less known destinations have risen to fill the gap including countries in the Americas, the ex-eastern European block or – recently – South Africa.

There are two alternatives on how this pattern can conclude: automation or death. After some time overseas, the outsourcing organisation can evaluate if the function under question adds value being still relevant. If so, then the next step would be to re-implement it in a cost effective way at this time back home. As an example, a department that needed 100 people to operate, after a thorough consideration and redesign ended up requiring 20, which made it feasible to have it along the other departments of the company close to corporate headquarters.

The other alternative is death. This can happen when the outsourced function becomes irrelevant or obsolete because the technological landscape has changed or the orientation of the organisation does not need it any more. Employees on the other end of the outsource will most probably be assigned to a similar project.

HOW POLICE PEOPLE REACT

Police employees in the department being outsourced will either be let go or will be transferred to an another department which might possibly face the same fate in the future. The receiving end of the outsource will continue maintaining the situation until the outsourcing organisation no longer needs the specific function or decides to bringing it back home.

For most of them, the whole process is inevitable; business as usual. Some will either be transferred to an another department in their current company or seek employment to another company with similar structure where the same chain of events might be triggered. Taking into account that, in Police organisations, changes take a lot of time to implement these cycles, this procedure could go on for ever or at least for a full career covering the current generation of employees.

■

PROGRAMMING LANGUAGES AS CULTURE & ARCHETYPE INDICATORS

OFTEN WE OBSERVE professional developers disagreeing on the choice of one programming language or more precisely language and implementation framework over another. To the outside observer the discussion seems to revolve around discussing trivia, sometimes philosophical/esoteric or even "mine-is-better-than-yours", childish arguments. In the best case, it seems like a conversation initiator similar to people asking where they are from in an international gathering or which sports team they support.

PROGRAMMING LANGUAGES AS CULTURE INDICATORS

The first argument in this chapter is that the choice of programming language is a strong cultural indicator either for the person or for the organisation that a person works for. This decision is subconscious most of the time which results in people discussing corporate culture very often without even knowing it. This also includes choice not only of a specific programming language but also of assorted paraphernalia such as version control system, frameworks, issue tracker, build automation tools, and others or even absence of those. The statement "we do not use build automation here", for example, indicates a strong correlation with how the supported organisation sees itself as well as its place within the industry and also its relation to internal and/or external clients. If an organisation has teams which are allowed to make different choices, then these choices apply in isolation within that specific team.

Because of the large number of programming languages available in production settings world-wide, the thesis will be illustrated with some examples primarily from the World Wide Web technologies, aiming not only to create an exhaustive list, but also to illustrate the main points of the argument. A more general discussion with a broader scope is conducted in the next section. This section is also not so concentrated on the main Archetypes argument, instead, it sets the scene illustrating another aspect of the industry.

The primary web language by popularity is named PHP. From its conception, the aim of the language was to embed small pieces of programmatic logic within HTML pages. As the HTML plus code projects started becoming more complicated and web development a whole ecosystem, PHP semi-organically evolved to support these needs. That did not change the core of the projects involved with the language, which are mostly centred around content: news-sites, blogs, e-magazines, and very often e-commerce. As a consequence of the above, we would more often than anywhere else see PHP installations in places that are related to news, advertising, infomercials, selling physical or digital goods etc. As a result, PHP developers are usually part of a company where programming skills, although important and essential, are not the only or many times the strongest contributing factor in the company's offerings. Additionally, because the language is easy to start with and someone learning it can become semi-competent quite fast, it has attracted programmers that have various levels of capabilities or competence over the years.

Another oft overlooked paradigm is the .NET framework and the entire Microsoft ecosystem. It evolves around the entrenched doctrine in Microsoft that all products should be aligned and interoperate well with each other. It is extremely easy in the Microsoft world to have a web application producing Excel sheets or Word documents for its end-users. Consequentially, it is the platform of choice for large companies that need a large number of internal facing applications with the majority of their infrastructure not exposed to the public. An industry where the stack is dominant is the financial sector, in which a finance worker would like to be able to produce a Word document or an Excel sheet with diagrams in just a few clicks. Most of the time we find .NET developers working in the finance industry or ones where the majority of work occurs "inside the corporate firewall". Generalising this would lead to influences from those environments such as the certification mentality[1] or a doing things "by the book" approach.

Comparing .NET with PHP in strictly technical terms, there is nothing that could stop it from providing very solid solutions for content presentation or e-commerce. While the contrary might be true, since for example it would be easier to consume and transform a Microsoft Word document within its environment, it rarely happens.

---

1. This references the certification era of the late 90s, early 00s where there was a certification for every major component of Microsoft's, Oracle's, and then Sun's ecosystem to name a few. Certifications for developing .NET for Desktop, Java for Web, maintaining Oracle databases and so forth. For those that entered the industry afterwards, you don't miss much.

An ecosystem with a different approach is that of Ruby On Rails. Although its market penetration is traditionally less than 5%, it has managed to become the lingua franca of start-ups. This might be a consequence of the design decision of its founder, Yukihiro Matsumoto, who aimed to create a language that would maximise programmer happiness, hence productivity, which is something that many start-ups need more than a compliant code-base from certified professionals. Ruby's success might also have to do with David Heinemeier Hansson, the framework's creator, a publicly known image who generally promoted the language to the start-up community. One way or another, using Rails equals to a small technically oriented company moving with high velocity.

Having contemplated how the choice of a programming language gives us clues on what the company does and in which industry it operates, we will discuss how the same choice can indicate an IT Archetype.

PROGRAMMING LANGUAGES AS ARCHETYPE INDICATORS

The "technology adoption curve" graph is the main tool used to describe how a technology propagates from an initial concept stage up to the point when it is retired. The enhanced version of this curve looks like the typical statistical bell curve skewed towards the end: First there are the enthusiasts, followed by the early adopters, which in turn continue towards the middle, with the early majority and then the late majority. At the very end of the bell curve sit the last ones that will eventually adopt a specific technology, let's call them last adopters. They are those who at least, but not only, in theory pay the penalty for being left behind and staying out of touch with the contemporary technological landscape, with a same thing occurring to a lesser extent to the late majority. There is one difference though with the typical curve: the early adopters are split by the so called 'chasm'. Some technologies never receive enough traction so they get retired very early, close to their introduction, as they never receive wide enough adoption to become established. To name a few examples from the gadget world, think of personal assistants such as Apple's Newton or the first attempts of Microsoft in the tablet world. These two examples are easier to comprehend since with hardware there is a material representation of the actual technological concept. Technologies and concepts that are way ahead of their time also fall in this category; if the world is not ready them, they might have a premature death only to see something similar to them popularized some years later.

Commandos feel comfortable in the space that starts from the early adopters and the early majority of technologies, be it a programming language or a specific framework. This does not only have to do with the modernity factor or following the hype or trends, but that in these areas, by definition, is where solutions are being suggested to the most contemporary problems; the exact problems that Commandos are facing and trying to overcome. Also, being usually fewer in numbers, Commandos want the additional productivity benefits that each new paradigm usually provides. The problem with early adoption space is that there are not enough tools, training resources, knowledge in the industry or a big number of corner cases covered simply because nobody has discovered them yet. For a Commando, the positive aspects outweigh these negative ones[2] or the negative ones are not that harsh: if you can read the source code of the framework you are using then you do not need to enrol in a certification course where someone else will tell you how it should work.

---

2. There is a good analysis on Steve McConnell's "Code Complete, Second Edition", more details on Bibliography.

Similarly, Infantry prefer to live in the early majority, only observing the early adopter space without engaging with it. There, technologies have been proven and, as it usually happens, this is the where many tools of integrating them with the existing infrastructure are introduced. The industry picks these up, salaries rise and the risk is considerably less. There are still some challenges but these are justifiable. Also, the people that would pay the Infantries to work in their companies do not need to be convinced of the benefits of early majority technologies, since this has already been demonstrated by the Commandos in advance while some crucial technological problems have also been solved.

There is a saying in the IT circles that a specific technology starts to become widely adopted once a big company embraces it or when a small company becomes big without changing it. PHP became an established programming language when Facebook went big and solved every possible scaling problem that language's implementations might have. The programming language Python[3] became popular after the rise of YouTube and Google. Ruby On Rails was used for the first years of Twitter, and the curious reader might come up with more examples. Once this happens, organisations start to want people to know these technologies which attracts professionals who want to pursue a career in these organisations. Hence a virtuous circle starts.

In the same fashion, Police people are more comfortable being in the late majority or in the last adopters space. This is where most people are positioned, the risk is minimised as all the major problems have more or less been solved, and there is a number of tools, material, and support available. If their technology of expertise gets retired, Police will move to another in the same adoption re-

---

3. "Python is a widely used high-level programming language used for general-purpose programming, created by Guido van Rossum and first released in 1991." (source: Wikipedia)

gion (late majority/last adopters). In between, they will benefit from the decreasing number of people skilled in these technologies, making the companies more dependent on them. As any company transition requires time, this guarantees years of job security to Police.

An illustrative Police example for non-web development could be Microsoft's Visual Basic. Once it was introduced, enthusiasts from all over the world could build applications for a desktop environment on the Windows platform overnight without having to take baggage with them from the command line environment of MS-DOS or the ageing Unix of the time. Sure, there were not many programming libraries available or books on the subject, but that was not a demotivating factor. Once Windows became dominant, many professionals started exploring this space and adapted the existing infrastructure, porting applications to the new environment or rewriting them from scratch. Visual Basic, being the popular kid on the block in the second half of 90s and also on the 00s, started falling from grace many years afterwards, once the .NET platform took over and there was more emphasis on the web. Long after this event, there is still a huge number of applications on which people depend, written in the latest iteration of the language (which is version 6.0) and a very big number of developers earn their bread and butter by maintaining and expanding these applications.

A similar situation holds for the once most popular business language, Cobol. People that mastered it in its glory years are securing their career sunshine and retirement package by maintaining legacy bank applications around the world, until a point in the future when fin-tech companies consume the market share of their employers or their employers acquire them. Policemen of the world unite!

This chapter is trying to illustrate a tendency rather than scientific proof, the number of examples was kept small to indicate a pattern. It might have to do with specifics of a programming language's design, or decisions made for web or other frameworks. Once a certain technology takes off, a different ecosystem and community spawns around it attracting similar minded people. Because this is not fully intentional, usually some of these choices or preference biases happen at a subconscious level. Hence, it is common for technical people to discuss and argue over the tools they use without knowing at the back of their minds that they are discussing their approach to work or what the company that they work for does.

■

THE TEN YEARS OF RAILS EXPERIENCE

IT WAS SOME TIME back in 2014 at a conference somewhere in the United States where the creator of Ruby on Rails gave a celebratory speech about the framework's ten years anniversary. One of jokes of his speech was something in the lines of: *"Now I am one of the very few people that can apply to that ad of Fortune-500-company-name-redacted which required 10 years of rails experience"*. Job postings like this, with different variations, happen all the time in the corporate world. Believing that it is an indicator of how a company approaches the capabilities and mentality of its employees, job postings will be treated as indicators of the current stage of a company and how it signals what type of employees it wants to attract.

FIRST WAVE, ZERO TO ONE POSTINGS

Companies on their first wave are more concerned about talent and character, hence their postings are mostly around these attributes. They might post a list of the technologies that are currently used but not so many details about level of familiarity or time spent with them. The reason is that this is what they need most: technologies as already discussed will most definitely change, what should be there and cannot be learned during the course of the employment is the approach towards the discipline. At the first stage of a company's life, this is the most valuable attribute and this is what is required.

For similar reasons, recruitment follows a more social approach than job postings in big sites. Networking is utilised more: companies reach people that the founders know personally or can be introduced from someone whose opinion they trust. An interesting synergy is with people leaving a company that has started moving towards its next phase, as described in the "Gentrification" chapter, being able to bring over their new experiences to the new venture. More often, recruitment process occurs in networking events in off-line settings. When on-line, more specific sites are preferred such as "Stack Overflow's careers" or others optimised for the specific profession such as "workshape.io" for developers or "Dribble" for designers. A recent trend is to monitor open source contributions and talk back to the people that facilitated them.

Another oddity is that many times companies are after the applicants, not the other way around which is the norm. This is because applicants are usually engaged with something so their time is limited, while at the same time the supply of candidates is less than the demand, so in order for recruitment to happen there is the need to engage with them.

IT recruiting for first wave companies is either facilitated directly from one of the founders or from the CTO. Knowing directly what they are talking about, probably having used it themselves, it is impossible to ask for ten years of experience on a framework that exists for the last five. The attitude and personality of the candidate matters more so the recruitment and interviewing processes are tailored accordingly.

SECOND WAVE, ONE TO TEN POSTINGS

In the same fashion, second wave postings reflect the status of the company. Companies on their second wave have stabilised on what they want to do and the people getting hired can now have a proper job description.

The second wave companies want to harvest productivity in a specific toolchain and experience on solving specific problems with it. The people compiling the advertisement are probably aware, at least empirically, of the results of that old study which stated that on a specific coding challenge: *"People with 10 years of experience did not outperform those with 2 years of experience. Only those with less than 6 months with the language did not do as well as the rest."*.[1] For this reason, the years of specific experience are toned down in something similar to: "at least two years of experience in deploying applications written in C#". Therefore, though general experience is important, there might be indicators of this such as: "senior developer" or "at least five years of industry experience", with the emphasis on the "industry".

Recruiting in second wave companies is usually conducted by the line manager of the open position which might involve CTO approval. It can happen through specialised channels and also networking. The ad post would be more easily seen in more popular internet locations though since the targeted audience is larger. Another source in the same area can be the product of scanning open source

---

[1]. Extract from "Peopleware", see bibliography.

contributions around the tool-chain that the company uses. A specific number of contributors can then be either contacted individually by, say, personalised emails or by an email campaign.

Ad postings are usually compiled from the line manager or a team member alongside with the Human Resources department or maybe a copy writer whose job is to make them more appealing. Usually they are a product of collaboration and proof read so it is not easy to ask for ten years of experience on a five year old framework unless it slips.

Second wave companies need the know-how of the applicant and her willingness to expand it in the areas that the company operates as a domain or technically, so the hiring process is concentrated around discovering these people.

THIRD WAVE, TEN TO HUNDRED COMPANIES

Third wave companies evolve around one criterion which is the holy grail for them and is no other than years on experience on the subject. So, a company at this stage would be mostly or only concerned around that.

Their rationale is that someone becomes more capable by working more and having years on the very specific job whose slot needs to be fulfilled. For example, a person that has four years of experience as a system administrator and two as a developer is a worse developer than someone that has never done systems administration and has developed for three years because three as a number is bigger than two. If the former one gets called for an interview in a third wave company, probably he will have to provide with some justification on why he did the switch: maybe he was not a good systems administrator in the first place. How do we know that he will not get bored with programming after some years?

Recruiting for these companies is usually outsourced to recruiting agencies that use general purpose recruiters or from the Human Resources department of large corporations. It mostly evolves checking against a check-list of corporate buzzwords doing a mix and match on CVs around the IT term or buzzword, years of experience and provided applicants' CVs triangle. The first person whose CV fits more the desired combination of skills is probably the best candidate.

For Ten to Hundred companies, CVs and overall traditional application process is their best choice as they do not understand the alternative methods or do not want to engage with them. Specific targeting is more of a luxury, similar to advertising to specific sites. Also the people that come from there are not a proper cultural fit, so it is better to avoid these channels.

A job posting for a such a company usually originates from the specific department and then progressively flows towards Human Resources. As human resources treat stuffing as their own domain for which they have full control, the posting can be altered at will without the need to ask the initial authors. This is where things can and usually go wrong because of the absence of a feedback loop. If we add some imperial arrogance from being part of an established and a rich company, things can get out of proportion. A possible trail of thought would be a senior programmer who has mastered a specific technology. But because we are talking about a fortune-100 company, then the applicants should be the best available where best, in our eyes, is measured by experience only. We then combine these two in "ten years of Rails experience" and the posting has the desired word economy.

■

TEAMS

LOOKING BACK at the previous chapters, the Archetype triad has been discussed concerning the specific people that constitute a company's workforce, and Companies acting as a whole or, as often mentioned, as an organization. From the organization's perspective, we have discussed the individuals, which are the micro level, the cells of a particular organization. And we have also discussed the whole, companies as single entities. What has been left out is the Teams that consist of individuals and form a working company. In the body analogy they would be the "organs" that together constitute the "organization".

There are many approaches to teams in the bibliography. The one most aligned with the Archetypes is the categorization of teams in Roy Osherove's "Elastic Leadership".[1] The three categories or modes are: "Survival Mode", "Learning Mode", and "Self-organizing Mode". The concepts of his analysis are "learning" and "slack time", which will be described along with the modes.

---

1. See bibliography for more.

The most common mode is having a team locked down in the Survival phase or mode. The title could but does not necessary have to imply people running round the clock, working long hours of overtime. Survival is described as the phase where a team does "not have enough time to learn" new skills. Teams in this phase are by nature reactive, do not develop the skills of their members nor can they plan ahead. Noting again that Survival mode does not necessary equal a high-stress working environment; most teams in the industry are in this mode with no inertia to move out of it. From an Archetypes approach, these would be described as Police teams since the way they solve problems or operate has a direct correlation. A phrase that is used to describe their day-to-day activities is "constant fire-fighting", which also constitutes the definition of a Policeman.

The next item in the taxonomy is for teams which are in the "Learning mode". A team is in Learning mode when it has "slack" time to learn new things and experiment. Learning and experimentation can be conducted either by concepts that are novel to the team or by spreading existing knowledge within the team. An example for the latter is teaching a new member how the building system works and letting them produce the next release's build. While in this case the concepts are novel to that particular member, they are not novel to the team. It could also be the case that a team member experiments with something completely new, which will then at a later stage be propagated to the rest of the team, if the experiment is successful.

The teams in Learning mode lean more towards the Infantry mentality than anything else. People that participate in these teams care about their professions and expand their skill set accordingly, learning from one another or from the scary Internet.

The third and last mode for a team is the Self-organizing mode whose leader has "grown the team to be self-organizing by teaching and challenging them to solve their own problems". A team in this mode can function without a team leader being present. It has specific goals and direction on what it has to achieve in order to support the organization and can move towards that direction independently. Its members can experiment, acquire new skills, make mistakes and correct them, realign the course towards the end goal. This behavior resembles what we have described as a Commando mentality.

The estimation of teams in Self-Organizing mode is at roughly 5% by the author of "Elastic Leadership". Surprisingly, the percentages are the same as the ones that have been suggested for people and companies: 80%, the vast majority, are in the Police/Survival mode either as a person or as an organization. A smaller 15% are in the Infantry/Learning stage, and 5% in the Commando/Self-Organizing stage.

SOME DIFFERENCES

The main difference between teams and individuals is that although an individual generally does not change orientation and approach throughout their career, teams can have so-called "shifts" between these three modes. Shifts can occur either by internal events such as team members leaving or joining the team or by external events such as changing commitments which impact the team's capability to learn or the time available to do so.

Another element is the presence of the team leader or management in general. While individuals act on their own or companies have a certain inertia and velocity that is difficult to alter, teams have managers or leaders whose personality or managerial style can have a tremendous impact on their course (hence the need to treat leadership differently).

NEXT CHAPTERS, WAY FORWARD

This is the last chapter in the second part of the book which expands on the principles discussed before, initially about the three Archetypes. The underlying concept of the second part was: if we try to see the corporate world and the world in general through the Archetypes lenses, are there any emerging patterns? Is it easier to explain "odd" behaviors and decisions of companies or departments with the Archetypes as a tool?

With the second part of the book being closely connected to the Archetypes theory, concepts presented in the following third and last part are more loosely connected and could in some cases stand as single essays or blog posts on their own merit. The benefit of having these chapters here is that the reader might approach them differently than when reading them alone in a blog post on a random website.

∎

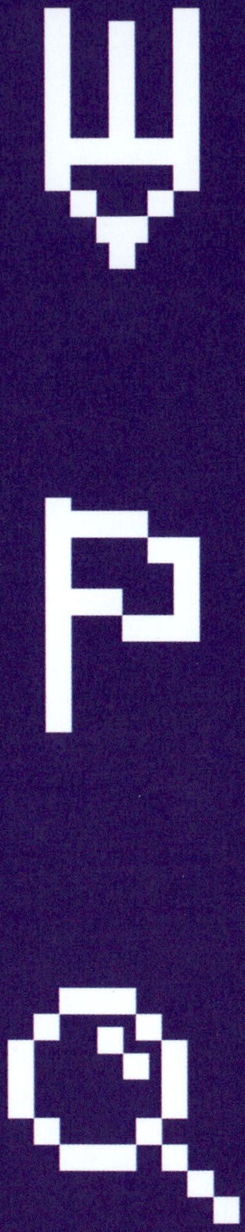

PART THREE

ESSAYS

SPANIARDS & ENGLISHMEN, MINDSETS, AND BLACK BOXES

HAVING DESCRIBED the different Archetypes, is it natural to ask about how these perspectives came into being in individuals or companies? Can a root cause analysis be conducted? There can be a number of answers from different angles involving sociology, psychology, education systems, family upbringing, and probably others. Three different approaches, from three different authors, will be presented. Surprisingly, although they have different starting points they seem to converge.

The common pattern in the subsequent analysis, from the IT Archetypes perspective, is that Commandos act in a specific way, Police in the opposite way to that of Commandos and Infantry somewhere in between by displaying mixing and matching behaviors with a dose of pragmatism and perspective which is the quality that distinguishes that Archetype.

ENGLISH VERSUS SPANISH APPROACH TO RESOURCE MANAGEMENT

There have been many references to the historical English versus Spanish approach since the distinction is very old. Here we will be more in the line with the "Peopleware" book which presents the argument specifically for the software/technology sector.

At some point in history there was competition among two approaches for acquiring wealth between those two corresponding empires. The Spanish approach advocated that the wealth on the planet was more or less a constant. As this theory goes the only way to acquire more wealth is by capturing or extracting as much as you can at all cost. This theory had a wonderful application when quantities of gold and indigenous people that were practically discovered overnight somewhere in the southern and central parts of the New World. The alternative was the English approach, which advocated that wealth could also be generated from better allocation of resources but mostly from technological applications and advancements. The juxtaposition of these two approaches comes up again and again, or to paraphrase the cliché, there is not exact repetition but certainly there is rhyme.

This perfectly fits the narrative about internal corporate structuring: Companies with a Police approach, usually in their mature phase of their life, try to improve themselves by creating an environment of resource extraction: do as much as you can with what you currently have, as it is being done already. The approach can be soft and encourage aiming at providing incentives or bonuses for working additional hours, or it can be harsh by having the time-keeper manager, who counts how much time each person is in the office, timekeeping when people go to the bathroom. When a company is on an expansion phase, most of the time it will be in a horizontal fashion trying to hire more people, creating additional managerial structures to accommodate for the additional personnel count.

Companies following the "English" approach aim to constantly improve their current position either by introducing new methods of solving problems or by developing their own innovative solutions to their problems. The output of their existing resources can be increased either by investments in infrastructure or by improving their managerial style. Similarly they are willing to expand the capabilities of their people for the same reasons.

MINDSET

"Mindset, How you can fulfill your potential" by Dr. Carol Dweck describes two distinct approaches: the fixed and the growth mindset. Quoting the author's summary:

"In a fixed mindset, people believe their basic qualities, like their intelligence or talent, are simply fixed traits. They spend their time documenting their intelligence or talent instead of developing them. They also believe that talent alone creates success — without effort. They're wrong.

In a growth mindset, people believe that their most basic abilities can be developed through dedication and hard work — brains and talent are just the starting point. This view creates a love of learning and a resilience that is essential for great accomplishment. Virtually all great people have had these qualities."

According to Carol Dweck the choice of mindset affects and very often determines one's work approach, ethics, decision-making process. Choice of mindset can occur either through education, the way someone was raised in childhood, or in our area of discussion, corporate culture. Although there are specific applications for companies, sports teams, relationships and other aspects of life, the underlying themes are approach to failure and growth. What follows is an attempt to map the mindsets to the Archetypes used throughout this book.

It is possible for a person to switch mindsets, although the forces that pin a person to one are usually hard to break. One can move from a fixed mindset to a growth one, once exposed to the theory, by consciously deciding to adopt it. Another person might start with a growth mindset and then gravitate towards a fixed one because of environmental pressure or a trauma. Or some people might adopt a fixed mindset for some aspects of their lives, a growth one for others. The situation for each person is not static but dynamic and fluid.

COMMANDOS - FULL GROWTH MINDSET WITHOUT LIMITATIONS

Commandos are positioned in the growth mindset camp. There might be a new technology in the market or a different approach or they might need to venture in a new field. They can jump ship and start learning, growing their capabilities until they become competent. They are not afraid of losing face or feeling "dumb" because learning is not just a part of what they do - it also defines who they are.

The fact that a novel approach might be a better fit for the problem at hand is treated more as an opportunity than a hindrance. Having been through the process of skill acquisition more than once, fear of learning something new has evaporated which allows the commando o constantly try to find ways to expand their capabilities and skill set.

Trying something that might not work as expected or even work at all is an exercise that enhances the mental capabilities of the participants. They can then go back to how things were before more assured that they should stay that way for the moment. If something did not work well, it probably did not work for them, it might be OK for someone else or for a different situation in the future.

INFANTRY - GROWTH WITH A SPEED LIMIT

Infantries lean more towards a growth mindset in an approach that advocates that growth is possible albeit within certain limitations. People can learn additional skills or reinforce their current ones within a process that is definitely slow and gradual.

As an example, every once in a while academics or journalists conducting research inform us that the amount of programming languages a developer can master during the course of his career is a specific number, usually three or sometimes four, or also that each developer stays within a specific ecosystem of operating systems or frameworks. This fits with a slow and gradual skill acquisition approach: learning the first one which will require a considerable investment in time and then moving on within a gradual process that takes years, as a limited growth mindset would allow.

Treating growth as gradual and as a generally slow process of learning, capability expansion should generally be well thought out and planned beforehand. Each person needs to have a very good understanding and a high level of certainty of future returns before trying something new. If something does not work out, then the time vested is considered time lost or wasted. Because of this, it is better to be conservative in setting targets. This can create fear which is projected into aphorisms such as: "this technology will never take off", or "this approach will never apply to our industry".

POLICE - STRICTLY FIXED MINDSET

For the Police mentality people possess a specific amount of capability that stays more or less constant throughout their professional life. The only thing that makes sense in such a reality is exploiting those limited resources as much as possible.

The idea of growing is frowned upon, treated like a Don Quixotian pursuit which is futile by definition. People that want to expand their skills are treated as if they want to avoid actual work, to be lazy or play - a counter-productive exercise.

Fixed mindset managers treat activities related to growth as "luxury" or as some sort of a devious trick that in the end makes people work more, a devious trick aiming to cheat workers into believing that there is an alternative or a different world "out there". "Company X", they tend to say, "does not have a different structure under the hood, all the "perks" that you see are a trick to make you want to stay in the office more, while I am letting you go after only 10 hours per day. As for the productivity enhancements, they just get graduates from the best universities of the country, unlike you or me".

Another consequence of the fixed mindset is the constant fear of failure. Failure in a business setting translates to the belief that the person was not good enough or has reached some arbitrary level of competence. The organization can have no benefit from a failed experiment or learning process, it just has to suffer from the time and money lost and so people and processes are geared towards minimizing everything that might introduce any risk which will eventually lead to failure.

A way to shield from failing is by doing the same thing over and over again, maybe with minimal variations or micro-adjustments. It is usually what made each individual succeed or what has been assigned by the company. The description above is perfectly aligned with the narrative of the Police-style mentality in people and in organizations. Employees are allocated to specific silos, conducting the same or as similar as possible tasks with potential small variations during their professional appointment.

THE INTELLECTUAL LIMITATIONS OF FIXED MINDSET

The fixed mindset mentality cannot explain where those fixed skills come from in the first place: Is it something that happens at birth, in school, or do they get forged in the university years? If the qualities and the level of a person are predefined and constant, how did that specific person acquire them?

The same question can be asked about well-established companies - if they are in a specific position in their market, how did that happen? Didn't someone in the past try something new, take some risks, offer an alternative or disruption to the market as it was back then? And if this is the case, is not someone doing the same thing by disrupting the currently fixed mindset company? In essence for a fixed mindset organization new skills or approaches have an aura of magic and rarity. It is mostly something that happens somewhere else, be it somewhere else on the Internet, in academia, or in mega corporations such as Amazon/Microsoft/Google. The only way to acquire them is to buy them through hiring or training, never produce them in-house.

OPEN AND CLOSED LOOPS

The last approach comes from Matthew Syed's "Black Box Thinking" whose first part explores different approaches to failure, mostly at an organizational /

professional level. Early on comes the distinction between an open and a closed loop system[1]: "*a closed loop is where failure doesn't lead to progress because information on errors and weaknesses is misinterpreted or ignored, an open loop does lead to progress because the feedback is rationally acted upon*".[2] Open systems accept the fact that they are imperfect, that failure will at some point occur and when this happens it will be a starting point for investigation, self-reflection or some sort of action that will eventually result in improvements of the system in question. Open systems are willing to adopt solutions that are relevant to them and would allow them to improve over other systems. The prime example used is the aviation industry where an accident is followed by experts conducting investigation and research which will then trigger policy and equipment changes so that the probability for a similar accident will be lower. This is where the "Black box" term refers to, to the box[3] that airplanes have, recording communications and information about the airplane. This would align with the Commando archetype in a more radical way and Infantry for a more subtle approach. Persons and companies in that stage would conduct policy reviews, post- postmortems or other activities that would eventually result in changes in their behavior and improvements in their products or services.

On the contrary, in closed loop systems there is the belief of self-sufficiency which rejects any form of feedback. People participating in closed systems treat errors as "one-offs" or incidents that happen from time to time which are statisti-

---

[1]. The terms Matthew Syed mentions originate from systems theory and engineeringbut for his book's purposes, hence here as well, there is a slightlydifferent meaning.

[2]. Quote on (1) from "A routine operation chapter", page 15 on UK version.See bibliography for more details.

[3]. Trivia: Contemporary "black boxes" are now colored orange. Again as in (1) it is not the engineering term as in "black box testing".

cally insignificant. There is sympathy for the participants that, according a closed system, happened to be unfortunate or in a bad circumstance. Matthew Syed then describes some mechanisms of how this happens, with two of them being re-framing and cognitive dissonance.

The closed loop system approach reflects the mentality of which we have associated in our narrative as Police-style organizations. When something does not fit the established world view, it is suppressed, ignored, or rejected pushing back with adherence to the existing procedures and operational mode.[4]

∎

---

[4]. This is not the theme of the whole book only how the author's researchbegins.

COMMANDO FOR EVER / ALTERNATIVE COMPANY STRUCTURES

A TOPIC DISCUSSED often has to do about the possibility of having companies remaining in their initial phase for ever, or perpetuating it as long as they can. There are two schools of thought on how to do this: there are some companies that believe that after the "Zero to One"/Commando friendly phase reaching the subsequent one is inevitable in a similar way as the phenomenon of aging in humans and other animals. With that approach trying to avoid this course would be similar to defying the laws of gravity. What a company can do though is age gracefully, or try to avoid as many undesired side-effects as possible. The other school of thought inspired by a more recent approach, believes that the inevitable corporate aging is a result allowing a specific type of environment that promotes specific behaviors to be created. By utilizing alternative organizational structures, companies can grow and scale up without becoming dinosaurs in the process. Let's examine some of these companies and the approaches that they followed.

DON'T GROW - IT'S A TRAP

Without mapping to a specific company structure, it is an approach worth considering. Some companies have decided to stay small in order to divert the side-effects of big monolithic companies. One of those could be the one run from the authors of "Rework" and "Remote", 37signals. When the company grew to a specific size, with their set of offerings starting to diverge serving different market segments, they decided to sell out one of the products and spin off another with to a different company.

The gist of this approach evolves around keeping the company small so that it can operate optimally, grow slowly and if things start getting bigger, split. By allowing people all over the world to work for the company working remotely and by sponsoring the - famous in web development circles -Rails framework, the best developers in the world want to work for them and also they can choose only the best ones since they are not hiring in large numbers and can filter out a lot before a hire. In the archetypes spectrum this approach could be translated as hiring only Commandos and maintaining a small surface.

VALVE

In the Valve universe the employees are allowed to switch projects and teams at any time they see fit. It's hierarchical structure is described as "flat". This goes so deep that even the employee handbook desks are equipped with wheels so that you as an employee should *"think of those wheels as a symbolic reminder that you should always be considering where you could move yourself to be more valuable."*

The Valve approach involves contemplation and) experimentation with core concepts of capitalism and interactions that happen within a free market zone. In order to study these elements they hired an in-house economist who blogged about the company's structure with some of the findings are available on their website.[1] An important note is that although many companies compete in theory within free markets, internally they look more like a Soviet state where corporate life is dictated by brutal rules and corporate state imposed monopolies. People although hired from the open market are then assigned to a manager which they can never leave unless there is a restructuring or an external event, managers cannot compete for talent. So if someone ends up with a manager who does not do his job well or just get along, she will have to wait some months or years for the opportunity to move. Similarly, teams or functions cannot request services only from within the internal monopolistic appointed departments: you need task management software? This has to go through the IT department which will force you to use the software tool that everybody else uses, whose vendor has a contract with the company. If the team requires specific features that another product does better, then they will be either "persuaded" to continue with the existing software or possibly initiate a long and arduous procurement process.

Valve solves the above by allowing and encouraging free flow of people within departments. Managers have to be good, projects need to be engaging and interesting or else people will move on to something else. The system is being guarded from company's founders and other "deities" that work and interact within the organization on a day to day basis.

---

1. http://blogs.valvesoftware.com/economics/why-valve-or-what-do-we-need-corporations-for-and-how-does-valves-management-structure-fit-into-todays-corporate-world

Criticism that this model receives is that it is difficult to scale Valve's model to a large number of companies or industries. The criticism is based on the assumption that Valve can hire the best people in their industries. They also happen to be self motivated or as this book suggests Alphas or Commandos so there is no need for external supervision. Another one is that the company's size is small: Valve has approximately about 500 employees which, although small for General Electric or Samsung standards, is probably above average for the software industry.

AMAZON

A company that follows some of the concepts of the Valve model is Amazon. There is some controversy about the way Amazon operates and treats its employees, but it is accepted that it has made the right choice on the following: the whole Company is structured in a way that each department works individually from the other ones offering services more or less as an external vendor would do. This allows the company to scale internally up and down as demand increases or decreases for specific services. If something does not work out, then it can cease without affecting the rest of the company. Equally if a department, for example shipping, performs well then it is ready to be open to the public allowing an additional source of profit and also as it scales cheaper services for its internal customers.

SPOTIFY

The criticism of Agile as a methodology is that it cannot scale as the company grows becoming a large entity. Spotify has succeeded in scaling up the Agile process in a company that not only is significant in its head count, but also spans along different cities and continents.

In Spotify, teams are arranged into small multi disciplined units that are called "squads". These units act like small start-ups working on a specific area at a time. Within them they follow the Scrum methodology. Ideas on what a start-up should work on are being generated from internal company "hack days". As products of those small units become more mature, they get introduced to the final product being progressively visible to internal, alpha, beta users and so forth. If an experiment succeeds it is being progressively rolled out to the end users allowing better scaling planning and management. If an experiment fails, it is being progressively removed.

These teams are supported and monitored from the rest of the company so that some side-effects can be handled like two teams working on the same team or one team depending on another one for features or resources.

As Conway's law on modular programming states: *"organizations which design systems are constrained to produce designs which are copies of the communication structures of these organizations"*. Consequently Spotify heavily uses service oriented architecture and the product is highly modular.

Spotify succeeded in pioneering scaling up Agile and ideas from start-up theory such as the minimum viable product. This happened because the company decided not to grow following the established mentality but rather walk its own path.

HOLACRACY

As stated: *"Holacracy is a new way of running an organization that removes power from a management hierarchy and distributes it across clear roles, which can then be executed autonomously, without a micromanaging boss."*. Placed here for purposes of completeness. What distinguishes Holacracy from other approaches is that its inventors decided to try to come up with a supporting theory and management frameworks on how to implement it, differentiating this approach from ad-hoc experiments that once they succeed then the organization tries to derive a theory in order to sustain them.

INVERTED/UPSIDE DOWN PYRAMID

Initially suggested by Joel Spolsky the man behind Stack Overflow, Trello and FogBugs. According to Spolsky most companies are being managed with the "Command and Control" approach where the higher echelons of each organization, the ones on the top of the hierarchical chart or the pyramid, make decisions which then have to be executed no-questions-asked from the echelons below. In some cases there might be some space for feedback or disambiguation but more or less the lower echelons blindly obey orders. It is called "Command and control" because it stems from traditional military.

The assumption on which this approach is based is that in the modern technological landscape the people closer to the real problems are the ones that are positioned below in the pyramid: It can be the developers that are having issues with a specific vendor or have to balance between specific and vague business rules. It can be the people on the support that sense that the end users find the current user interface hard to use.

The suggestion is to inverse the pyramid: hire the best people that you can and let management instead of ordering, support them into making the best decisions possible for the company. Management's role should be to support their teams so that they can perform as effortlessly and optimally as possible.

Quoting an illustrative example: *"When two engineers get into an argument about whether to use one big Flash SSD drive or several small SSD drives, do you really think the CEO is going to know better than the two line engineers, who have just spent three days arguing and researching and testing?"*. In this example the role of the management is to provide with direction and specifics of the problem that needs to be solves such as "we need to figure out how to store X type of data on Y volume" and enough information, "we need to increase the speed of data retrieval". Then being in the same example management should provide the necessary equipment required to run those tests, an environment where the two developers can exchange ideas and decide for the best interest of the company without punishing the one who lost the argument. Once they reach to a conclusion their manager's role should be to assist them on finding the appropriate hardware vendor.

In a nutshell this approach emphasizes supporting modern knowledge workers into doing their job.

GOOGLE

Google seems to have some elements from the inverted pyramid. Google's strategy evolves around hiring the "best" people it can in every country/area that it operates. Then these people are provided with everything that they need to do in order to work without distractions supported a system that provides everything that they might need such as the well known high quality food, health care, eye tests, equipment, backup equipment while equipment might be repaired and so forth. People are allowed to ask questions and there is an air of transparency. All the elements that a person would need to perform are there. Google has been criticized for the lack of feedback loops specially in the higher levels of its management, for example, its co-founder Larry Page being in denial about the fact that products such as Google Plus were not getting traction. Apart from that fact Google's model answers to the criticism on scaling because of the company's size which is approximately 100 thousand people including temporary workers.

More than anything else Google has proven that a company can effectively battle decay and stay "Commando" for many years indicating that there is a paradigm shift, not some blips or exceptions on the traditional organizational model.

STEVE JOB'S NOT TIM COOK'S APPLE

Main point of reference is Steve Blank's post "Why Tim Cook is Steve Ballmer and Why He Still Has His Job at Apple".[2] In essence there is one visionary CEO, such as Jobs, that runs the company. The main function is to see the future, articulate it to his subordinates who then are responsible for executing his ideas, manifesting them into reality.

This process if it is repeated constantly over time keeps the company always into the forefront of the industry and shields it from irrelevance. For Apple's case it would be: iPod, iTunes, iPhone, App-store, iPad, and so forth. None of these products or services are fully exploited financially, as effort is shifted not to optimizing sales channels or generally execution, but innovating on the next area. Of course people would be assigned into the existing areas, but the whole company's

---

[2]. https://steveblank.com/2016/10/24/why-tim-cook-is-steve-ballmer-and-why-he-still-has-his-job-at-apple from Blank's personal page, or https://hbr.org/2016/10/why-visionary-ceos-never-have-visionary-successors which is the Harvard Business Review version. There has been lots of material about late Steve Job's management and approach, but this specific article aligns perfectly with the subject of this chapter.

focus would be something else.

The issue identified by Blank is that such momentum is very difficult to maintain once the visionary innovative CTO steps down. Being the center of the universe, his immediate subordinates, the C-board, consists of execution oriented people, which makes them by definition not a good replacement. The successor should be either elected from a person sitting lower in the organization's hierarchy or from outside. The norm though is to elect someone from the C-board, such as Tim Cook for Apple or Steve Ballmer for Microsoft, who will then focus on execution and maintaining "what we already have achieved", while in parallel allowing the organization to lose it's identity and edge.

∎

WHY GOOGLE

THIS CHAPTER'S PURPOSE is to provide an answer to the question on why people want to work for companies in the likes of Google, Twitter, Facebook, but also Spotify, Twillio, Paypal and Microsoft. An alternative way to phrase the same question is "what makes these companies so different?".

I believe that many of those differences stem from the fact that their founders are almost always engineers which is probably a very important factor. Another one of not so significant importance, but nevertheless important, is that many of those had a first generation immigrant on the founder team.

FOUNDERS ENGINEERS

Recent founders from engineering background introduced two elements that generally did not exist at least not extensively in the corporate culture of many companies. The first one is the belief that good companies are not created spontaneously but are a product of iterative social engineering. As engineers are supposed to change or tweak computer programs or designs, in the same fashion company structures and corporate culture can be improved on a all levels - a jargon term for this process is "hacking corporate culture". This contradicts two popular opinions on the issue: One says that once companies reach a specific size or after some years are more or less immutable and can only be managed. The other one is that the only way to facilitate change is by changing leadership and which then will issue big "corporate memos" similar to imperial mandates of ancient emperors, or their email equivalent. So it is not the case that Sergey Brin wakes up one morning deciding on the way to the office that dress code should be more relaxed, then sending an email to everybody expecting that by next week everybody will be wearing hipster t-shirts. Constantly evolving through countless iterations is something that can and should be done, definitely in the realm of possibility.

Another contributing factor that originates from the engineering disciple along with the constant disruption that those companies face, is the conscious attempt understand and reverse the processes that makes companies stale and become conventional (or stupid or boring). Alternatively they might adopt a proactive approach identifying and limiting the forces of decay or experiment on alternative approaches to management. From the many examples the most appropriate one is Spotify, which has as a company succeeded in scaling up agile system. Another company that has achieved this is Valve, the owner of the Steam gaming platform. Google used to have the 20% free time model, followed up by bold movements and experimentation on different areas: Internet provider form a Zeppelin or the self driving car.

Believe that these are the archetypal reasons that manifest on a day to day level on the reasons why "Geeks" want to work for them so much, this is what is discussed in the following paragraphs, not in a particular order of importance as this varies per person.

COOL FACTOR

One aspect should be the feeling that "what you do matters". The product of your work has a direct impact on the industries that those companies operate sometimes also reshapes society and you are a part of that. Strong sense of mission and purpose.

Another aspect that has only recently started to be discussed on articles and blog posts is the so called "cool factor", something identified in the past but recently gets progressively more and more attention.

As the narrative goes, many people that later became engineers had a rough time in school moreover in high school period of middle and late teens. This is a period that stigmatizes life with effects that for many people can endure forever. Traditionally the scientific person in the classroom is usually classified as at least not-cool if someone prefers mild wording or geek for the less political correct audience. Generally children that ended up computer scientists behaved historically different than the norms and got ignored or at least misunderstood. Sometimes their dress-up can also be different/unconventional or below standard maybe because they invest their free time occupied on scientific matters or just because they do not know better. There might be boyfriends and girlfriends but definitely not in the number of hundreds that the "popular" kids have or enjoy being in the spotlight. Spotlight is usually reserved for the athlete, the bimbo, the stylish one not that much for our little engineer to be. All the above are could be OK but definitely not pleasant. Until it becomes too much either through ostracism or some acts of bullying that targeting our teenage subjects of discussion is introduced to the narrative.

As our analysis goes these experiences either traumatic or not follow those people later on. Some remain more thirsty for coolness some not that much. For the still thirsty ones joining one of those companies acts as a baptism in cool-aid / purification ceremony if such an analogy is appropriate. As the priest baptizes you in holy water and cleanses you from cardinal sin, joining one of those companies cleanses the non-coolness away, but not only that: as an added bonus you get additional celebrity capital. This celebrity capital can be used either for healing the existing traumas or for being popular in the present, perhaps to potential romantic endeavors.

It is uncertain where the cool factor stems from but it definitely exists. Maybe it has to do with the brand name, or the fact that they can hand pick their employees making it difficult to join. For an average layman it could be that their product of service is used in every day settings, it is a household name. Alternatively there can be a fear element: the power of a company that annihilates many traditional businesses. As Niccolò Machiavelli wrote hundreds of years before *"it is better to be feared than loved"*?

COOL FACTOR AND STICKERS

Ending this long part allow an additional anecdote involving… stickers. While working in Accenture employees were assigned company laptops. A question came up: *would anyone place an Accenture sticker in his corporate or personal laptop*? The answer is probably not, put there the logo of a … consultancy? Would a Google sticker land on your laptop? Easily yes. The computer currently used to write these lines has one with the logo of a JavaScript framework I am using, Firefox web browser's logo (my favorite browser), flags of the countries that it has traveled and a motivational quote from Startup vitamins.[1] This was realized when I saw that the Google's corporate laptops from Google where branded, not only to be recognized them on a client setting, but also because the employees were not only comfortable but proud to have them along in public settings. This could also be the case companies such as Twitter or Twillio. The organization does not have to be huge, Twillio being a perfect example, but it needs to have that cool factor. So if you see your company logo ending up on people's laptops, Moleskins / notepads, congratulations you are popular!

BREAKING THE CHAIN OF PROGRAMMER'S LIFE CYCLE

Next comes the promise of eliminating "boredom". Before discussing boredom it should be defined for our context, which is the one defined from Russell Ovans. Quoting his article[2] on the subject, at some point our workers reach the state of boredom": *Bored. The post-resentment equilibrium sees the programmer's activities shift more towards ongoing maintenance, consultative meetings with management, and internal knowledge transfer to other programmers and customer support staff. Because the initial challenges of the new project, environment, and technologies have all been met, the intellectual stimulation has dropped. This leads to boredom.* The important word in our case is "maintenance" as the state of when there is not anything new to discover learn or exper-

---

[1]. "Get S**t done" for the curious reader.

[2]. "The programmer life cycle", http://www.goodreads.com/author_blog_posts/2036266-the-programmer-life-cycle

iment with. For most people this is equal to a state nirvana, because there is no stress involved, not in our case though.

I have experienced two transitions of companies from the start-up to the typical boring company stage, one of them violently. Specially on the violent one, before transitioning I was engaged, enthusiastic, happy - waking up early and thinking about that great thing that could start once I sat on my desk on the one hour-long commute to work. Just one week after the transition I responded by becoming a typical corporate zombie. Hoping that it would take some months for management to realize it, had that time used not for finding my next position and also negotiating employment terms. Everything seemed to follow Russell Ovans' pattern.

Many people have shared same experiences sometimes in a smaller scale but nevertheless more often than someone would initially assume. One similar pattern is discussed in Wassermann's "Fouder's dilemma" is the "congratulations, you are fired" concept. There the company has discovered it's business model, consequently the stabilization activities start: Freeze innovation, stop the spontaneous interactions between departments - become "boring" at all costs. This affects engineers in multiple levers: what interests them, what they like, what they are good at and not least what makes them important is just no longer relevant. Only option for them is to start looking for the next thing.

The companies we are discussing established that if a specific department reaches this stage, the programmer's life circle can restart internally, eliminating the need to refresh one's CV and change jobs. Some examples include rotation to similar teams or being assigned to a completely different team and then get back (example: a graphic designer following for the sales team for a while receiving valuable insight on how clients actually use their design). If nothing else at least arrange some time for open source contributions. Engineers feel that they will stay there for long. Their families have less worries about them moving places and associated risks that come this might bring.

MERITOCRACY AND LESS OFFICE POLITICS

Next factor should be the hope of meritocracy or at least meritocracy to an order of magnitude above the average. As it has already been mentioned for a variety of reasons including projections of one's beliefs or education, most technologically oriented employees assume some sort of rationality affecting the structuring and everyday operations of companies. This naivete gets crushed from office politics, corporate backstabbing, gaming the system in order to be promoted, stealing other people's work and so forth. What is more puzzling is not the individual incidents of these behaviors but why companies or organizations allow them in the first place.

These companies project the census that employees will be evaluated from their work alone or at least more then from a conventional company. It might be due to their affiliation with data and information processing or maybe because they have been founded and run by engineers who somehow try to engineer a different environment. It might be that they actively try to be small or have few hierarchical layers which makes it easier for each type of behavior to be visible.

In order to illustrate the previous argument, a story that circulated news sites can help involving the Google Marissa Mayer while still in Google and an unnamed graphic designer. Although there is a strong tendency to side with the designer, it illustrates the previous points: Graphic designer was defending his choices on a page layout based on aesthetics, business practices and taste. This was paradoxically contradicting usage data that was collected from real users of the system. Mayer was forcing him to reconsider based on these data. As the story goes the designer was so pushed and the directions that were so against his approach that on the end he decided to quit. Although it seems so difficult not to side with the designer (even Google changed it's mind some years later on this approach) what signifies this story is the fact that the company was trying to find an objective measure of what is "right", in that case measured user behavior. Although someone might disagree on the appropriateness of those criteria, it is not difficult to agree that this is way better than appointing a "user representative grand-master" with dictatorial power over user interface decisions, basically projecting his opinion or that of the people he favors.

LAST BUT NOT LEAST

As a last remark something that should not be left out is momentary compensation. One justification has to do with a way more than average revenue per employee. It can be easily assumed that this allows for higher compensation and other benefits the so called perks. The argument of course is that the whole structuring of those organizations exponential productivity which in turn allows higher incomes which then end up to compensation schemes. So last but not least we can "follow the money".

These are some answers to the question on why many people want to be in one of those companies, try hard and get upset if they get excluded as we can read in random ferocious blog posts.

■

BIBLIOGRAPHY

1. "**Accidental Empires: How the Boys of Silicon Valley Make Their Millions, Battle Foreign Competition and Still Can't Get a Date**", Robert Cringely. http://www.cringely.com/tag/accidental-empires/

2. "**Brave new world**", Aldous Huxley.

3. "**The founder's dilemma**", Noam Wasserman, Princeton University Press. Statistics and analysis from a large sample of start-ups and technology companies, and also transitions such as the "congratulations you are fired". http://www.noamwasserman.com/book/

4. "**Zero to One**", Peter Thiel. http://zerotoonebook.com/

5. "**Handbook for new employees**", Valve Press. http://www.valvesoftware.com/jobs/index.html, http://media.steampowered.com/apps/valve/Valve_NewEmployeeHandbook.pdf

6. "**Peopleware: Productive Projects and Teams**", Tom DeMarco & Timothy Lister, John Wiley & Sons. An online version of a previous publication available here: http://javatroopers.com/Peopleware.html

7. **"Founders at work"**, Jessica Livingston, Apress.
   http://www.foundersatwork.com/

8. **"The programmer life cycle"**, Russell Ovans, http://www.goodreads.com/author_blog_posts/2036266-the-programmer-life-cycle

9. **"Steal Like An Artist"**, Austin Kleon, Workman. Not used for this book as any way but included as an honorary mention because Austin Kleon's book provided the mental authority to be able to "steal" from the references above. http://austinkleon.com/steal/

10. **"Mindset, How you can fulfil your potential"**, Dr Carol S. Dweck, Robinson/Hachette. Referred while discussing mindsets of archetypes or companies, http://mindsetonline.com/thebook/buythebook/index.html

11. **"Black Box Thinking"**, Matthew Syed, John Muray / Hachette UK. Referenced while discussing the open/closed loop approach chosen from archetypes or companies, http://www.matthewsyed.co.uk/blackboxthinking/

12. **"Transactional Analysis Theory: the Basics"**, Carol Solomon. For stages of companies and internal communication processes, http://www.carolsolomonphd.com/web_pdfs/Transact.pdf

13. **"Rework"**, Jason Fried, David Heinemeier Hansson. Referenced in the "Commando for ever" suggesting different ways of company structuring and operations, https://37signals.com/rework

14. **"Code Complete, Second Edition"**, Steve McConnell / Microsoft Press. Chapter 4, section 3 titled "Your Location on the Technology Wave" has a very good analysis on choosing a technology stack, http://cc2e.com/

15. **"Elastic Leadership**, Growing self-organizing teams", Roy Osherove, Manning. Basic point of reference for the "Teams" chapter is the second chapter titled "Matching leadership styles to team phases"

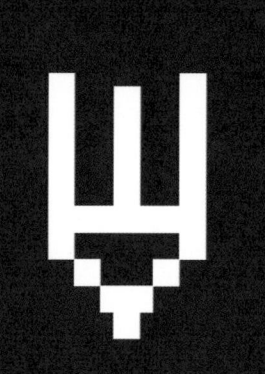

AUTHOR

Dimitry is just your next door computer geek. After many adventures in IT land he decided along with a band of friends to tell his experiences so that other geeks will benefit from them. Follow him on Twitter @dimist and check his website: www.mistriotis.com

Printed in Great Britain
by Amazon